Cost-effectiveness and independent living

Proceedings of a JRF seminar, June 2000

Edited by Alex O'Neil and Janet Lewis

Frances Hasler, Ann Macfarlane, Steve Martin and Howard Davis, Gerry Zarb, Sarah Byford and Ann Netten

The **Joseph Rowntree Foundation** has supported this project as part of its programme of research and innovative development projects, which it hopes will be of value to policy makers, practitioners and service users. The facts presented and views expressed in this report are, however, those of the authors and not necessarily those of the Foundation.

Published for the Joseph Rowntree Foundation by YPS

ISBN 1 84263 025 3

Cover design by Adkins Design

Prepared and printed by:
York Publishing Services Ltd
64 Hallfield Road
Layerthorpe
York
YO31 7ZQ
Tel: 01904 430033 Fax: 01904 430868 E-mail: orders@yps.ymn.co.uk

CONTENTS

LIST OF PARTICIPANTS

Terry Bamford	Independent consultant
Ian Basnett	Camden & Islington Public Health Department
Louise Brown	R&D Partnership, University of Bath
Sarah Byford	Centre for the Economics of Mental Health, Institute of Psychiatry, London
Jane Campbell	National Centre for Independent Living
Clare Evans	Wiltshire & Swindon Users Network
Frances Hasler	National Centre for Independent Living
Ann Kestenbaum	Independent Living Fund
Martin Knapp	London School of Economics
Janet Lewis	Joseph Rowntree Foundation
Ann Macfarlane	Disability consultant
Steve Martin	Warwick Business School
Ann Netten	Personal Social Services Research Unit, University of Kent at Canterbury
Alex O'Neil	Joseph Rowntree Foundation
Hazel Qureshi	Social Policy Research Unit, University of York
Michael Turner	Shaping Our Lives
Gerry Zarb	Freelance disability researcher

INTRODUCTION

This publication reproduces the papers for (and some of the discussion that took place at) an expert seminar organised by Joseph Rowntree Foundation during June 2000 on cost-effectiveness. The seminar was prompted by a number of concerns and ideas that were current in the Foundation's Social Care and Disability programmes. It also happened at a time that the Foundation was starting to address wider issues of cost-effectiveness in social policy more generally.

Issues of cost and effectiveness are particularly relevant to current wider policy and practice issues. The Labour administration came to power in 1997 with a strongly expressed interest in evidence-based policies. The present initiative of Best Value gives expression to this concern; the intention is to see practice as being developed, not on the lowest cost option, nor simply on being delivered by the competition of the market-place, nor even through the achievement of greater efficiencies. Rather, the intention is to have a clearer idea of the aims of public service initiatives and evidence for how these might then be achieved through more effective delivery.

These (more macro-political) concerns are also evident in social care and disability issues. Many recent Foundation reports, particularly within its Independent Living programme,[1] have identified specific issues, especially in relation to the way that costs and effectiveness are addressed.

- Although the culture in social care has been changing over the past decade, there is still a lack of more quantitative, robustly comparative cost and financial data about support to older people, disabled people and service users more generally.

- This lack of data can mean that incorrect assumptions are made, about the costliness and effectiveness (or otherwise) of more traditional and of newer types of services. In local and national projects about direct payments, for example, many local authorities started from the doubtful presumptions that direct payments schemes would be more expensive and less reliable than their own in-house services.

- Most especially, there still remains little clarity about ideas of 'effectiveness'. The dominant thinking is still to deliver a traditional and fairly formulaic idea of (e.g. domiciliary) services at the lowest cost.

- Although ideas of user involvement are acknowledged, there is still little involvement in defining ideas of effectiveness, 'outcomes' or quality.

The above issues present challenges to how cost-effectiveness can be *formulated*, even before embarking on challenges of *measurement*.

Beyond the Foundation's projects, there were already expressions of interest and concern to reframe ideas of cost-effectiveness. It was decided to ask key stakeholder groups within each of the main constituencies (the disabled people's movement, among academics and among those concerned with development and implementation of policy and practice) to present some initial thoughts on how cost and effectiveness might be taken forward.

The process of the seminar was, therefore, twofold. The first was the preparation of the papers from each of the stakeholders (revised versions of these papers are included in this publication). The second was to discuss the implications of the papers with representation from each of the constituencies, and more specifically to address three key questions.

- Does it seem feasible and desirable that value-bases such as Independent Living can be used as central to the definitions of 'effectiveness' and 'outcomes'?

- What is the state of play in the formulation of the tools of cost-effectiveness? More especially, is there a feasible formulation of cost-effectiveness that is both reasonably robust and attainable?

- Finally, could the group start to work towards next steps on how useful ideas of cost-effectiveness might be taken forward?

In the papers that follow, *Frances Hasler* and *Gerry Zarb* and *Ann Macfarlane* present overviews of the foundations of and current issues within independent living. They outline the application of this philosophy to current ideas of service delivery and of direct payments to disabled people, and also some of the issues in applying this philosophy to the lives of other groups, particularly older people. A paper by *Steve Martin* and *Howard Davis* outlines the current state of play (in policy and practice terms) of Best Value; *Gerry Zarb*'s paper presents a critique of the ideas of Best Value and argues for a framework which takes forward ideas of cost-effectiveness within a value-base of independent living. Papers by *Sarah Byford* and *Ann Netten* look to focus on the specific approach to cost-effectiveness that would be feasible, given our current state of knowledge, and then to develop practicable approaches to building a framework for cost-effectiveness within social care and disability issues.

Note

1   For example, publications from recent JRF reports:
    Bignall, T. and Butt, J. (2000) *Between Ambition and Achievement: Young Black Disabled People's Views and Experiences of Independence and Independent Living.* Policy Press
    Butt, J., Bignall, T. and Stone, E. (2000) *Directing Support: Report from a Workshop on Direct Payments and Black and Minority Ethnic Disabled People.* York Publishing Services
    Clark, H. (forthcoming) *Help not Care: Extending the Philosophy of Independent Living to Older People*
    Dawson, C. (2000) *Independent Successes: Implementing Direct Payments.* York Publishing Services
    Holman, A. and Bewley, C. (1999) *Funding Freedom 2000: People with Learning Difficulties using Direct Payments.* Values Into Action
    Kestenbaum, A. (1999) *What Price Independence? Independent Living and People with High Support Needs.* Policy Press
    Zarb, G., Campbell, J. and Hasler, F. (1999) *Direct Routes to Independence.* Policy Studies Institute

PART 1

DISABLED PEOPLE AND INDEPENDENT LIVING

1 Cost-Effective Support Within a Framework of Independent Living – Principles of Independent Living

Frances Hasler and Gerry Zarb

Introduction

The first part of the paper sets out the principles of independent living, as defined by disabled people and their representative organisations, and draws on research evidence on what constitutes quality outcomes for independent living. Following on from this, the essential features of independent living are contrasted with current definitions of community care and the reforms proposed in *Modernising Social Services* (Department of Health, 1998).

The principles of independent living

Article 1 of the International Covenant of Civil and Political Rights states that everyone should have the 'right to self-determination and to freely pursue their economic, social and cultural development'. Without independent living many disabled people will never enjoy that right.

Independent living is the emancipatory philosophy and practice which empowers disabled people and enables them to exert influence, choice and control in every aspect of their life.

3

The essential principles of this emancipatory philosophy have recently been re-stated by an international convention of disabled people and can be summarised as follows:

> "The basic principles of Independent Living philosophy are human rights, self determination, self help, cross disability (i.e. including all sorts of impairment), empowerment, inclusion, risk taking and integration.
>
> "The Independent Living philosophy recognises the importance of accepting responsibility for our own lives and actions and at the same time the importance of community to foster independent living.
>
> "We recognise the importance of equal and inclusive education, employment opportunities and entrepreneurship, personal assistance, assistive technology, accessible transport and a barrier-free environment to promote Independent Living."
>
> (*The Washington Declaration*, prepared by delegates from 50 countries at a global meeting in September 1999)

There are three constant factors in disabled people's definition of independent living:

- It is owned by disabled people – the concept was developed by and for disabled people.

- Equal opportunities and social inclusion are integral to the definition of independent living: 'enabling choice and control cannot be exclusively for one impairment group or age group in our society' (Mason, 1999).

- The social model of disability provides the philosophical framework for the definition of independent living.

Independent living means different things to different people. However, two defining concepts mark independent living from other approaches to meeting disabled people's support needs:

- *choice* over where to live, how to live, who provides assistance

- *control* over who assists, and how, when and what they do.

In the context of social services and community care, the main vehicles for promoting independent living are personal assistance and direct payments schemes. *Personal* means that users exercise maximum control over how services are organised, and custom design their services according to their individual needs, capabilities, life circumstances and aspirations. *Assistance* is used to indicate the relationship: this is not 'looking after' a disabled person, it is working with him/her on his/her terms. A personal assistant will perform all the required tasks that a disabled person is physically or intellectually unable to do in order that the person can achieve his/her goals.

Direct payments were developed to enable disabled people to get personal assistance (although in the UK they can also be used to provide transport, equipment, advocacy or other services if these are within the scope of local community care policies). They are therefore a crucial component of any policies aimed at supporting independent living.

What constitutes quality support?

As we have already noted, disabled people's definition of independent living as a way of meeting support needs centres on the concepts of choice and control. Previous research on the costs and benefits of payments schemes and services, and on independent living and older people indicates that these two core concepts are also reflected in how disabled people define the quality of their support arrangements (Barnes, 1997; Zarb and Nadash, 1994; Zarb and Oliver, 1993).

Control over the times support is provided allows people to have more control over their own time and gives greater continuity to the pattern of day-to-day life; it also makes people's support arrangements more reliable and, therefore, reduces stress and anxiety.

Control over who is employed includes being able to have a choice about support workers' characteristics – particularly age and gender and, where applicable, ethnic or cultural origin; also the power to apply direct sanctions to ensure that staff deliver assistance in an appropriate and acceptable way.

Control over how assistance is provided helps to ensure that support is given in the most effective way. By this we mean that it is closely matched to individual needs and preferences. Control also has wider benefits in terms of enhancing personal freedom and dignity.

Reliability is also a key indicator of quality. Reliable support arrangements not only increase confidence but also create greater freedom for people to arrange their lives to suit themselves. For some people (particularly older people), reliability is also closely linked to the issue of safety.

So, in the context of independent living, quality support can be defined as support that offers:

- choice and control

- reliability (both in terms of individual workers and of continuity of support)

- flexibility

- personal freedom and dignity (sometimes described as 'autonomy')

- choices about how people live their lives

- safety and security to remain living in the community.

The Department of Health funded research programme on outcomes of community care has also looked at some of the broader issues around what disabled people and other groups of service users see as appropriate outcomes for support systems, and how these should be assessed. Some of the main conclusions from this research included the following (Nocon *et al.*, 1996):

- There should be a focus on higher-level aims such as enabling people to participate fully in the lives of their communities, rather than simply keeping them clean and fed.

- Quality is not only about inputs and outcomes. Process issues, such as relationships with staff and support workers, and the degree of control which users are able to exercise over services, also need to be integrated with consideration of outcomes.

- In addition to the immediate and practical outcomes of support services, attention also needs to be paid to wider 'distributive' outcomes such as fairness and equity.

Community care or independent living?

The ideas informing independent living and community care are sometimes quite different from each other, as the comparison between personal assistance and care shown in Table 1.1 indicates:

Table 1.1 Key characteristics of social support and community care

Personal assistance/social support	Care
Practical assistance with day-to-day activities	Palliative treatment/health care
Caring about (part of normal family and social relationships)	Caring for (a purely functional relationship)
Interdependency and reciprocity	Dependence
Chosen (and in case of assistance controlled) by disabled person	Designed and managed by others
Enabling social and economic activity	Assuming lack of economic activity; limiting social activity

As a result of these fundamental differences, independent living struggles to grow in a framework of social welfare that is often in direct opposition to it. The basis of community care is meeting professionally defined 'needs' in a 'homely' setting. User choice should be sought but does not have to be respected if giving the user what she wants is not considered to be 'cost-effective'.

As we have noted in the past:

> "The essence of independent living, as defined by the disability movement, is that people should be enabled to define their own needs and how these should be met. The concept of community care also includes maximising choice and flexibility as one of its central objectives. Under community care, however, needs are still essentially defined by enabling authorities. Further, as any form of community care provision is subject to the availability of resources, the process of assessing and defining also inevitably involves a process of rationing these resources between competing claims."
>
> (Zarb and Nadash, 1994)

Further, there is a major disincentive for disabled people to engage in economic activity. The current system of charging for non-residential community care means that people with income over the basic income support level are being expected to contribute varying, but often quite large, sums to the cost of that care. This has several effects. For many older people it means going without something else in order to pay for the care, or foregoing the chance of care because of fear over the cost (Chetwynd et al., 1996). For younger people it can mean giving up opportunities to work, as all of the fruits of the efforts will be taken up in care costs, leaving them no better off than if they did not work. This has important implications for the issue of defining cost-effectiveness, which we will talk about in more detail later.

In addition, practically all of the existing support systems place some kind of ceiling – either in terms of cost or eligibility criteria, or often both of these – on the level of resources at which community-based living is deemed to be viable. This means of course that people for whom this is not considered to be cost-effective are faced with a stark choice between struggling to maintain their independence in the community, or entering institutional care. Effectively, this amounts to putting a price on people's lives. No amount of rhetoric (however well intentioned) about 'enabling', or 'empowerment' and so on will disguise this (Zarb, 1998).

So, while government guidance is exhorting local authorities to ensure that services enable social and economic activity, the reality is that they are often planned and rationed on a basis that does the opposite.

Of course, one of the main reasons why this state of affairs still exists is that there are a number of competing pressures on scarce resources. Despite general agreement about the desirability of promoting independence, fears still remain that wholesale investment in independent living could divert resources away from other areas of need which, by implication, are seen as more urgent. However, as we have argued before:

"... the fact that people who use payment schemes often depend on the assistance purchased for their survival means that there is an inherent (and powerful) incentive for them to use this money effectively. If they may sometimes choose to purchase alternative types of assistance which are not easily available through service provision, this would normally be because this is seen as more appropriate to their particular needs. So, putting the issue the other way around, it could be argued that – rather than diverting resources away from other areas of need – direct payments actually represent a more efficient way of targeting limited resources."

(Zarb and Nadash, 1994)

Modernising social services

As noted earlier, the values of independent living are increasingly accepted, even if practice has still not caught up. Organisations with responsibility for providing social services are now willing to sign up to a broad range of independent living goals. The Association of Directors of Social Services, for example, recently issued a joint statement with the Direct Action Network which included the following points of agreement:

- all assessments should start from the position of a personal self-assessment contributed by the disabled person

- social services to work to ensure that every disabled person has a choice not to live in an institution

- try to ensure that the social model of disability becomes the core value-base of social work practice with disabled people.

There are also signs that a broader, more enabling, definition of independent living can – in principle at least – now be incorporated into the mainstream of social services policies. The white paper, *Modernising Social Services* (Department of Health, 1998), includes the following as one the National Objectives which local authorities need to take into account in the implementation of Best Value:

"To promote the independence of adults assessed as needing social care support arranged by the local authority, respecting their dignity and furthering their social and economic participation."

(Department of Health, 1998)

Interestingly, for the first time, this 'mainstream' definition of independent living explicitly acknowledges the wider objective of enabling social and economic participation – which, at least in its terminology if nothing else, is much closer to a social model definition than we have seen in earlier policy statements. This is also underlined in the Guidance for local authorities on how to evaluate their progress towards achieving the objective of promoting independence in the context of Best Value performance reviews:

> "Setting objectives for social services within a corporate framework of the council's overall objectives for its local people should enable local authorities to consider the way in which social services interact with other local authority services, such as education and housing. Some authorities may wish to tackle these issues through cross cutting objectives relating to particular user groups, e.g. services for older people or youth justice services, rather than objectives for single services."
>
> (Department of Health, 1999)

Again, the reference to the interaction between social support and education and housing indicates a broader view of independent living, and a recognition of the fact that enabling real independence involves tackling disabling barriers across the board. A companion paper by Gerry Zarb in Part 3 of this report looks at how this objective might be translated into the evaluation of cost-effectiveness and Best Value.

Bibliography

Barnes, C. (1997) *Older People's Perceptions of Direct Payments and Self Operated Support Schemes.* Leeds: University of Leeds

Chetwynd, M., Ritchie, J., Reith, L. and Howard, M. (1996) *The Cost of Care: The Impact of Charging Policy on the Lives of Disabled People.* Bristol: The Policy Press

Department of Health (1998) *Modernising Social Services.* London: Stationery Office

Department of Health (1999) *A New Approach to Social Services Performance.* London: Stationery Office

Mason, P. (1999) 'Back to basics', in NCIL *Facing Our Futures – The Short Report.* London: NCIL

Nocon, A. and Qureshi, H. (1996) *Outcomes of Community Care for Service Users and Carers: a Social Services Perspective.* Buckingham: Open University Press

Nocon, A., Qureshi, H. and Thornton, P. (1996) *The Perspectives of Users and Carers Organisations.* Outcomes in Community Care Practice Series No. 4. York: Social Policy Research Unit, University of York

Qureshi, H. and Nocon, A. (1995) *Key Issues in Outcome Measurement for Practice.* Outcomes in Community Care Practice Series No. 1. York: Social Policy Research Unit, University of York

Zarb, G. and Oliver, M. (1993) *Ageing with a Disability: What do they Expect after all these Years?* London: University of Greenwich

Zarb, G. and Nadash, P. (1994) *Cashing in on Independence: Comparing the Costs and Benefits of Cash and Services.* Derby: BCODP/PSI

Zarb, G. (1998) 'What price independence?', in M. Turner (ed.) *Facing our Futures.* London: NCIL, 1998

2 INDEPENDENT LIVING FOR OLDER PEOPLE

Ann Macfarlane

"Grow old along with me, the best is yet to be."

In our current society, Robert Browning's words do not seem to hold much truth. The question is can we work together to give them more resonance for people as they grow older?

This paper will focus primarily on independent living in relation to older people. It will explore what needs to happen now and in the future to make independent living a real and meaningful experience for people in these groups. The term 'older people' will be used throughout the paper. It will also make reference to the needs of black people and people from minority ethnic communities, and, where there are issues in relation to black people and people from minority ethnic communities, this will be stated.

One of the current problems in talking about independent living for older people is that older people themselves, professional people and the disabled people's movement have different, and conflicting, understandings of what independence means.

For example, to determine independence, professionally trained people often undertake an assessment process based on physical or mental functionality. Older people themselves often concur with this approach, which mostly leads to the provision of pre-designed services. For example, isolated older people may receive a day centre placement, frozen meals, or personal care from teams of carers.

In contrast, the disabled people's movement defines independent living as being in control of your own life. In practice this often means choosing who helps you, how, where and when. For each individual, independent living may alter over time as the person makes changes in their life, as they grow and have different experiences. Here is what independent living means to three recent direct payments recipients:

Example 1: Until recently, Jenny has been supported within her family with little opportunity to take risks. Aged 25, she now has her own flat. Her greatest achievement and greatest struggle was to make a cup of tea with help from her personal assistant. She does her own shopping, chooses sandwich fillings and makes sandwiches for her college lunch box. Soon after moving she tried out a local disco and, instead of her personal assistant staying, she was provided with a mobile phone so she could gain personal assistance if required. Opportunities to enjoy the risks and experiences of non-disabled peers are and will continue to be part of Jenny's empowerment process.

Example 2: Florence is a disabled mother with a two-year-old child (Simon). Florence has gained independent living through a Disability Facilities Grant that enabled her to have her kitchen adapted. The Social Services Department arranged for a through-floor lift to be installed which means Florence has access to Simon's first-floor bedroom, can oversee his bath-time routine and read him his bedtime story. A personal assistant helps Florence to take Simon to and from school and with school activities.

Example 3: Fred, aged 74, has been living on his own for three years. Both his visual and hearing impairments are deteriorating. He likes cooking and uses personal assistants to assist with reading recipes and preparing dishes. He also likes shopping for clothes and, as he is on a low income, enjoys bargain hunting with the support of a personal assistant. Reading and responding to correspondence with personal assistance has become less daunting and maintains Fred's privacy.

These examples show that independent living is about an individual's own judgement of what is important to them. Disabled people access independent living *through personal assistance.* This is support for one individual alone, arranged by the disabled person to meet their needs. This might be practical assistance, i.e. cleaning, driving, personal help, help with going out or assistance with childcare.

This relationship between a disabled person and a personal assistant is based on working with the disabled person on their terms; it is not about *looking after* or *caring for* the disabled person.

Mike Oliver summarises the independent living philosophy as follows:

"Central to this philosophy is the issue of personal assistance which is necessary for disabled people to participate in all of the activities of everyday life and includes work, leisure pursuits, education and personal relationships. Choice and control are key factors in this participation and disabled people must exercise both of these in making decisions both about their personal assistance and the activities in which they wish to participate."

(Oliver and Postance, 1996)

For older people and people from black and minority ethnic communities, much of what has been said about independent living may apply. However, unfortunately, these groups have traditionally been excluded from the debate. It is possible to catch some glimpses of what independent living means to older people. Research undertaken by Heather Clark *et al.* (1998) reveals that older people view remaining in their own home as marking the final boundary of their independence. 'At home, you can control what you do, when and with whom.' They made a clear distinction between being *at* home and being *in* a home. Older people defined personal assistance as *help* not *care*. They wanted services that supported them to care for themselves.

Further, older people appeared able to shift their boundaries in relation to independence. Mrs Jones moved into sheltered accommodation when her husband died because she could no longer manage her home and was nervous of living alone. She didn't consult her family about the move because she liked to retain control. She defined independence as: 'I like to be able to manage on my own for as long as I can and as well as I can.' The help she now required with vacuuming and laundry didn't undermine that 'because I need it'.

It is apparent that the definition of independent living, as provided by the small number of older people consulted, has principles in common with those defined by the disabled people's movement and these will be explored later.

But who are 'older people?'

What is meant by the term 'older people?' Government policy determines 'older people' by chronological age. For example, the state pension is available to women at 60, and to men at 65, and the Attendance Allowance can be applied for when a person reaches 65. Voluntary sector organisations may determine the age of 50 as being 'older'. Insurance companies may decide on several different age brackets and premiums to determine when older people can expect to receive a retirement pension, money for health requirements or for accidents acquired when travelling.

Again, however, the views of older people themselves are missing from the debate. There is a lack of consultation on this subject. Almost all policy making, research and writing on older people's issues has been undertaken by younger, non-disabled people. That means assumptions are made.

Perhaps one way older people can be defined is through the concept of 'life changes'. Getting older is a time when children have become of an age and left home, when a career or paid work has ended, or when leisure or sports pursuits have become too demanding and something less fatiguing is required. It is a time when older people may leave their home and move to smaller or sheltered accommodation. It might relate to them losing a partner and finding bereavement overwhelming, or when financial circumstances change and their circle of friends diminishes. Life changes relating to the older generation can come within a wide time frame and may determine when a person feels 'older'.

One way out of the conundrum of how to define older people is that older people should determine when they acquire the label in much the same way that disabled people decide that they are 'disabled.'

Further, whilst it is clear that many of the policies and practices that discriminate against disabled people also impact on older people, their situations are not directly comparable. There are differences. Older people may lose their health, physical and mental abilities may deteriorate, partners may die and peer groups diminish. There is little mileage in applying theories of discrimination unthinkingly to these issues.

However, the ability to go out, participate in community and leisure activities, and enjoy accessible housing are issues where discrimination and oppression can occur and these must be challenged and changed.

The key principles of independent living

One way of examining how the key principles of independent living, as defined by the disabled peoples' movement, can inform the debate on older people is to state them very clearly.

1 Many of the problems older people face are discrimination and oppression issues outside of themselves and their own bodies.

2 Older people have the right to represent their own interests.

3 Older people have the right to assess their own needs.

4 Older people should not be divided by impairment or age.

Each of these will now be discussed in turn.

First, many of the problems that older people face are discrimination and oppression issues outside of themselves and their own bodies. This approach to disability was historically developed in the late 1960s and in the 1970s. Disabled people living in long-term residential settings made a bid to escape, fighting against segregated provision and financial charges for services. Collectively, disabled people began to join forces and set up Centres for Independent Living – places where disabled people could gain information about housing, transport, educational opportunities, training and advocacy. They fought for the right to live independently in the community. Part of the route to this freedom and liberation has been achieved by campaigning for direct payments legislation.

Older people have not joined in the debate for this liberating form of provision. They have fought for services that have emerged following the Second World War, services that would support them in later life. They fought for services free at the point of delivery. Those services included general and specialist hospital provision and community services. Since the inception of the welfare state, services have become more professional, dividing people by age, impairment and culture. When older people have been referred between specialist services, professionally trained people have further separated and segregated them. These separations isolate older people but this does not deter them from asking for and demanding these traditional forms of support. What has emerged from specialist provision is difficulty in allocating and moving financial and human resources.

So, whilst viewing disability as discrimination may be applicable to older people, it is important to recognise the different histories of older and disabled people's political involvements.

Second, older people have the right to represent their own interests. Tessa Harding summarises the overall situation for older people as follows:

"If all older people are being offered are the high cost, high dependency services, then that, eventually, is what they will be forced to use. A national strategy is needed to turn this situation around and to support the independence and inclusion of older people. Such a strategy needs to be comprehensive, not piecemeal, and to address the needs of older people in the round."

(Harding, 1997)

She concludes:

"Older people have a key role in formulating such strategies, since they know better than anyone else what it takes to retain health, autonomy and inclusion in society in older age."

However, Vincent (1999) notes:

"Not only do older people not think and act as an interest group, but also they do not organise effectively to focus objectives and achieve them. Even taking into account their difficulties of physical mobility and resources, older people do not mobilise militant support in the manner of road protesters, animal rights or disabled activists."

These problems need to be addressed for any substantial moves forward to be achieved.

Third, older people have the right to assess their own needs.

The voluntary sector has a dynamic role in contributing to the development and delivery of services with older people. Small, locally based services make a big difference, for example, befriending minority ethnic communities. It is vital to harness the energy and expertise of older people who can provide advocacy and information.

The Anchor Research document states:

"It is important to work with local older people to develop an overall vision for the lives of older people which encompasses their whole range of needs and aspirations and to seek to shape a culture sensitive to these. There needs to be recognition that older people often have the resources and will to manage their own solutions to their problems if provided with appropriate support and opportunities."

(Lewis *et al.*, 1999)

Fourth, we must ask whether it is helpful to continually divide older people by age or impairment. The disability movement has fought for older people to have access to direct payments. However, there seems to be little understanding within the older people's lobby for the importance of such divisions to be broken down. The best example is of the carers' movement where older people have been driving a movement that has been based on dividing disabled people and their family members or friends. This is a movement that continually and negatively portrays disabled people as burdens. Such regressive political approaches must stop.

Policy

Does the current policy framework at a national level create an environment in which the lives of older people can be improved? I would argue yes.

First, it is the Government's aim to make policy making more strategic, by producing policies that are:

"... forward looking and shaped by the evidence rather than a response to short-term pressures; that tackle causes, not symptoms; that are measured by results rather than activity; that are flexible and innovative rather than closed and bureaucratic."

The focus of all disabled and older people's policies and strategies should be on social inclusion and fair access. These policies and strategies require the development of joined-up objectives between departments, and should demonstrate Best Value in service planning and provision.

Second, one of the main problem areas, that of long-term care, has had some solutions. The Royal Commission on Long Term Care suggests that the cost of care for those individuals who need it should be split between living costs, housing costs and personal care. Personal care should be available after an assessment, according to need and paid for from general taxation; the rest should be subject to a co-payment according to means.

The report also raises the issue of older people who require limited amounts of support in order to stay in their own home but, due to restricted local authority financial resources, are not eligible under current assessment arrangements. There is high value in low-level preventative support and, because older people are often denied this, they end up requiring high levels of support following a crisis. Low-level direct payments can be highly effective!

Third, there is a range of initiatives attempting to listen to older people. For example, over the last two years, Age Concern launched 'Millennium Debate of the Age', Help the Aged, 'Speaking up for our Age' and the Inter-ministerial Group, 'Older People's Listening Events'. Better Government for Older People, which works to a national steering committee, aims to raise the profile of older people by giving them a greater say at national and local level. It has spearheaded 28 pilot projects across the country and the outcomes are due to be published in June of this year. At least half the projects have directly focused on consultation with and the involvement of older people, including those from minority ethnic communities.

Fourth, Best Value allows us a mechanism to review services and practice.

Lastly, the 1999 Health Act that came into force on 1 April 2000 allows new powers to enable health and local authorities to work together for customers' interests with pooled budgets, lead commissioning and integrated provision. These new powers can lead to creativity, and can include housing, transport, leisure, library and other community services.

What needs to be done now?

Three approaches would help develop better provision for excluded groups: first, the creation of an environment where younger individuals, couples and families can practically prepare for old age; second, consultation on services for older people must engage with younger constituencies now; third, the principles of independent living must be used as a toolset to change traditional forms of provision.

The following two examples compare the situations of one person who has planned well for their old age and one who has not.

Example 1: Marjorie aged 90, became ill in her late 70s and was in bed at home for four months. She had never before been in hospital or experienced ill health. As she had no family to attend to her needs, a neighbour supported her on a regular basis. When health returned, Marjorie determined to sort out her future. She had visited a number of friends in residential settings. They had suggested that she consider placing her name on a waiting list for the group of homes they were living in. Two years later she moved into the south London provision. Eighteen months after moving, Marjorie was involved in a serious accident, falling between a station platform and a train. She was in hospital while her injuries healed and was discharged to the nursing wing of the home. After six months she was well enough to return to her own room. The home failed to meet EEC regulations and had to close down. Marjorie moved to another home in the chain in Worcestershire, which she knew well. She has friends in the local church. Marjorie worked abroad, has friends worldwide and belongs to the International Organisation of University Women. Her mobility is impaired but she enjoys her room and gets on well with several people in the home. She contributes within the home and wider community, and recently made arrangements for herself and two other residents to learn about the Internet.

Marjorie's plans for her later years have worked well. She knows she can move between provision on the same site should the need arise. The home's financial policy is designed to ensure that residents enjoy a quality life style within their capabilities.

Example 2: Stanley is 88 and continues to live alone in the family home. His wife, Rose, to whom he had been married for 65 years, died two years ago. His physical and mental health has deteriorated and he has had several hospital admissions. He uses a walking frame to access the kitchen and toilet. He and Rose made financial plans for their older years but no decisions were taken about the management of their day-to-day existence.

Stanley does not want to go to a day centre and will not consider moving into a residential setting. He employs a home help for seven hours a week and a gardener for a half day each month, and accepts the help of a home care assistant for half an hour each morning and evening. His small circle of friends is drawn from the local church. He complains about and is confused by the increasing numbers of professional people entering his home. Like so many people of his age, he refuses to spend money on himself as he is saving it for the family and his old age!

These two studies illustrate how two people similar in age, health status and financial circumstances are dealing differently with their situation. Much will depend on financial circumstances, on living accommodation and the ability to move, on health, on whether there is a partner to provide support, and on family and community support.

Working with younger people now

Second, consultation on older people's services must engage with younger people. Becoming older and issues associated with death are slightly less taboo. Younger people are being challenged to plan for old age. Younger people do support older relatives and friends, and there is understanding of the lives and issues of older people. Younger people's lives are often different from the lives of their parents. Greater opportunities are experienced in terms of careers, travel and life style. Technological advancements have created higher expectations. This group will want to access:

- inclusive mainstream services
- good quality information
- personal assistance and direct payments
- travel in the UK and abroad
- shopping centres accessible by public and private transport

- opportunities to select, purchase and prepare food

- visits to and from family and friends

- computer and Internet facilities

- high-quality health care

- educational opportunities.

The small percentage of people who may opt for living in a supported environment are more likely to select quality hotel provision and use direct payments to pay for their personal assistance.

Applying the principles in this way might require a shift in resources from departments of social services across all local authority budgets. This would enable policies and practices to more appropriately reflect needs and result in inclusive mainstream provision.

Independent living principles must start to change traditional services

The disabled people's movement has worked hard to encourage individual disabled people to come together; it has supported groups of disabled people to empower themselves in order to get their voice heard. This has been and still is a struggle. Despite the existence of older people's groups and pensioners' forums, it is disabled people who have fought for older people to be included in the direct payments legislation.

People in their 70s and 80s have shown little interest in direct payments, and this is reflected in the fact that older people were not visible when disabled people were lobbying and campaigning for their inclusion in the legislation.

The Department of Health (1998, p. 18, para. 2.15), on making the decision to include older people stated:

"Direct payments are giving service users new freedom and independence in running their lives and we want more people to benefit from them. We have decided, therefore, to remove the age limit and to make people aged 65 and over eligible for direct payments."

Before the legislation was finalised, an as-if scheme was piloted in Portsmouth. It was set up as if direct payments were an option. It highlighted the difficulties that care managers experienced in discussing direct payments with older people, preferring instead to talk with carers and carers' groups. The Social Services Department advertised for and recruited personal care assistants, as they were called, and paid them rather than giving older people the resources. Older people were entitled to choose a personal care assistant from those who qualified to work on the scheme and the result was similar to receiving agency support. There is little experience of older people taking full control of the money to pay personal assistants and responsibility for employing them. In *Direct Routes to Independence* (Hasler *et al.*, 1999), research indicated that older people might require a slightly more structured support arrangement, which might include an advocacy element.

The majority of older people have not yet heard of direct payments but, where they have been considered or are an option, research has identified several issues.

Colin Barnes writes:

"Many of the concerns expressed were similar to those of younger disabled people and included the responsibility of administering a direct payments scheme, sorting out tax and national insurance and not having back-up in an emergency. The majority of older people wanted to be able to employ family members. There was great concern that existing services or financial benefits would be reduced or withdrawn. Older people in the groups, who were receiving indirect payments, had rarely experienced problems and were very enthusiastic about direct payments."

This indicates the need for greater numbers of older people who can act as role models and encourage positive images of independent living acquired through a direct payments scheme.

Direct payments appear the best option available to older people to support independent living. If that were so, what would make direct payments attractive to older people, as evidence shows that they are not coming forward to claim this option? This work needs to continue in local settings with new initiatives undertaken by the Department of Health.

Exploring direct payments and independent living within sheltered accommodation and residential and nursing home settings might be one way of making a difference to the lives of older people. An option might be to set up pilot sites to establish ways of working that are attractive to older people.

Those who are becoming older people will almost certainly challenge perceptions of older people and promote positive images.

To conclude

In developing policies, strategies and practices that embrace older people's aspirations and needs, it should be remembered that many of the problems they face are discrimination issues outside of themselves and their own bodies. Older people have the right to represent their own interests and assess their own needs, and impairment or age should not divide them.

Keeping these key independent living principles at the forefront of development and planning, older people may engage with Robert Browning's philosophical approach: 'Grow old along with me, the best is yet to be.'

Bibliography

Benington, J. (1997) *Local Strategies for an Ageing Population: The Need for Inter-agency Action.* Warwick University/Local Authorities Research Consortium

Blakemore, K. and Boneham, M. (1994) *Age, Race and Ethnicity.* Open University Press

Clark, H., Dyer, S. and Horwood, L. (1998) *'That Bit of Help': the High Value of Low Level Preventative Services for Older People.* Policy Press/Joseph Rowntree Foundation

Department of Health (1998) *Modernising Social Services.* The Stationery Office

Dunning, A. (1995) *Citizen Advocacy with Older People.* Open University Press

Harding, T. (1997) *Lives Worth Living – the Independence and Inclusion of Older People.* Help the Aged

Harrison, L. and Heywood, H. (1999) *Health Begins at Home: Planning at the Health–Housing Interface for Older People.* Policy Press/Joseph Rowntree Foundation

Hasler, F., Campbell, J. and Zarb, G. (1999) *Direct Routes to Independence: a Guide to Local Authority Implementation and Management of Direct Payments.* Policy Studies Institute

Hughes B. (1995) *Older People and Community Care.* Open University Press

Laurie, L. (1991) *Building our Lives – Housing, Independent Living and Disabled People.* Shelter

Lewis, H., Fletcher, P., Hardy, B., Milne, A. and Waddington, E. (1999) *Promoting Well-being: Developing a Preventative Approach with Older People.* Anchor Research

Macfarlane, A. (1996) 'Aspects of intervention: consultation, care, help and support,' in Hales, G. (ed.) *Beyond Disability: Towards an Enabling Society.* Sage

Morris, J. (1997) *Community Care: Your Rights to Housing and Support.* Pavilion Publishing

Oliver, M. and Postance, B. (1996) *Service User Involvement in the Development of Home Care and Agency Services.* Greenwich Joint Care Commissioning Council

Vincent, J.A. (1999) *Politics, Power and Old Age.* Open University Press

Zarb, G. and Nadesh, P. (1994) *Cashing in on Independence: Comparing the Costs and Benefits of Cash and Services.* BCODP/Policy Studies Institute

Zarb, G. and Oliver, M. (1993) *Ageing with a Disability: what do they Expect after all these Years?* University of Greenwich

Discussion

The discussion that followed the presentations by Frances Hasler and Ann Macfarlane centred on a number of key issues.

All too often, policy-makers and practitioners confused independent living with a mode of service delivery to people living in their own homes. Disabled people in the discussion said that this 'medicalised' idea of independence saw them as bravely 'struggling against adversity' towards an ideal where they were independent by doing everything by themselves. When this was not possible, they were seen as 'giving up their independence' and had then to allow themselves to be cared for by others, sometimes at home, sometimes in an institution. Such a formulation of 'independence' was not independent living.

The social model of disability, on the other hand, emphasised the rights of the individual to lead the life they chose, while being in control of the support needed to do that. That support could come in a variety of ways (e.g. personal assistants) and could (in theory) be achieved even within more traditional forms of service delivery. The key was about choice and control in practice.

In fact, there was a general and speedy recognition among all members of the group that independent living was about people having the support to allow them to lead full and independent lives. There was a general acceptance that philosophies and values similar to those of independent living should and could formulate the value-base of 'effectiveness' in social care and disability support. The real task would be to take philosophies of choice and control into practice.

In practical terms, other members of the group pointed out that resources were finite and that decisions would always have to be made about priorities. Disabled people acknowledged this. For some, it was about a rights-based approach, which identified equal, basic rights for everyone (which then needed to be resourced). For others, it was about the service user's views being paramount in how finite resources are distributed (entitlement) and then used (assessment). The central point was that a philosophy of independent living could still be applied in a world of finite and limited resources (though that should not be used as a pretext for defending inadequate resources).

Applying these ideas to the practice setting, disabled people said that the original language of community care was about choice and control only within a set of needs *predefined by the enabling authority*. Practice to date had been about increasingly tight rationing according to these predefined needs.

Moving on to the needs of older people and people from black and minority ethnic communities, members of the group then recognised that there were particular barriers within social care. There were many examples of these barriers. Access to (and the suitability of) services for black service users (or potential service users) was still problematic. The cost ceilings on support for older people were much lower than for younger people.

There were also similarities and differences in applying the concept of independent living for different groups of people. However, it was also possible that there was common·ground between older people and disabled people, as well as diversity among different groups and individuals.

In summary, future work on independent living and cost-effectiveness would need to be based on ideas of user choice and control. This would need to recognise that at present policy makers were not fully working within empowering models of user involvement. There were some hopeful signs in policy terms in current developments. However, the fundamental problem was about translating fine ideals into practice. At present, ideas of independent living were still not central, and the current economic tools to evaluate ideas of 'cost-effectiveness' or 'Best Value' were often simply a proxy for cost-minimisation.

PART 2

IDEAS OF BEST VALUE, COST-EFFECTIVENESS AND INDEPENDENT LIVING IN SOCIAL WELFARE

3 IMPLICATIONS OF THE BEST VALUE REGIME FOR INDEPENDENT LIVING

Steve Martin and Howard Davis

Introduction

This paper analyses three main issues:

- the development and implementation of the Best Value regime at national level

- the ways in which 'Best Value' is being defined and implemented at local level

- the extent to which the regime has led, or is likely to lead, to greater user involvement in service design and delivery, and the implications for independent living.

It concludes with some examples of early pilot reviews that focused on services for people with disabilities, and some practical suggestions for future monitoring of the new regime and its impact on independent living.

The Best Value regime

Best Value principles

The Best Value regime is the result of a commitment made by the Labour Party to repeal legislation requiring a range of local authority services to be subjected to compulsory competitive tendering (CCT). Its 1997 General Election manifesto stated that 'Councils should not be forced to put their services out to tender' but would 'be required to obtain best value' (Labour Party, 1997, p. 4). A month after coming to power in 1997, the Labour Government announced that it would be 'pressing ahead with its manifesto commitment to replace the failure of competitive tendering ... with a new duty for local authorities to ensure best value for the public' (DETR, 1997, p. 1). The then Local Government Minister stressed that the new regime would force all authorities to improve but emphasised the importance of service quality and the role of local people in reviewing standards. Achieving Best Value would 'not just be about economy and efficiency but also about the effectiveness and quality of local services. The new framework will be demanding ... seeking continuous improvements in service costs and quality. It will be a permissive framework which emphasises local choices and accountability' (DETR, 1997, p. 1).

The Best Value pilot programme

The Department of the Environment, Transport and the Regions (DETR) stated that the new regime would be introduced 'as soon as parliamentary time allows'. In the meantime, it invited local authorities in England to apply for exemption from CCT for activities covered under the 1988 Local Government Act in return for piloting the so-called '12 principles of Best Value'. In Scotland and Wales, where there was already a moratorium on CCT, all local authorities were encouraged to begin to adopt Best Value principles. More than 150 English councils applied to pilot Best Value. The 40 successful applicants were announced in December 1997. They included five county councils, 15 shire districts, seven shire unitaries, six London boroughs and seven metropolitan districts, plus two police authorities. They were drawn from all parts of England, proposed a diverse range of interpretations of Best Value principles and encompassed an array of different services (Martin, 1999).

The duty of Best Value

The pilot programme ran from April 1998 until March 2000. Just before it started, the Government issued a consultation paper (DETR, 1998) outlining in more detail its proposed approach to Best Value and describing the so-called 'Best Value performance management framework' (see below). The local government White Paper (Cm. 4014, 1998), published in July 1998, was followed by a Bill published in November 1998 and the Local Government Act that received Royal Assent in July 1999.

The Act requires Best Value authorities to 'make arrangements to secure continuous improvement in the way [their] functions are exercised, having regard to a combination of economy, efficiency and effectiveness' (HMSO, 1999, clause 3.1). The accompanying guidance states that they must fulfil this duty in accordance with the 'Best Value performance management framework'. This involves three main steps. First, establishing authority-wide objectives and performance measures. Second, agreeing and undertaking a programme of fundamental performance reviews. Third, producing annual Best Value performance plans (BVPPs) which are intended to act as 'the principal means by which an authority is held to account for the efficiency and effectiveness of its services, and for proposals to improve upon them' (DETR, 1999b, para. 43) and address the following issues:

- a summary of the authority's objectives

- an assessment of the level at which, and the way in which, the authority exercises its functions

- the timetable for conducting Best Value reviews

- a statement of performance indicators, standards and targets for each of the authority's functions

- a summary of the authority's own assessment of its performance

- a comparison of its performance with previous years and with the performance of other authorities

- a summary of the authority's success in meeting, or making progress towards meeting, performance standards and targets.

They are subject to external auditing and summaries have, by law, to be distributed widely. As with other elements of the regime, failure to comply can result in ministerial intervention and, in extreme cases, removal of functions from local authority control (see below).

Best Value reviews must cover all services, sub-services and other functions over a five-year period. They are 'designed to be the principal means by which authorities consider new approaches to service delivery and set demanding performance targets for all services so as to deliver continuous improvements' (DETR, 1999b, para. 16). Authorities must examine their objectives and assess their performance over time, in comparison to other service providers and against any performance standards and targets that have been established (HMSO, 1999, clause 4). Reviews need to:

- *challenge* why and how a service is being provided

- secure *comparison* with the performance of others across a range of relevant indicators, taking into account the views of both service users and potential suppliers

- *consult* local taxpayers, service users, partners and the wider business community in the setting of new performance targets

- consider fair *competition* as a means of 'securing efficient and effective services'(DETR, 1999b: para 16).

These so-called 'four Cs' lie at the heart of the Best Value process together with a fifth C – 'collaboration' – that was added in the 1999 White Paper on *Modernising Government* (Cm. 4310, 1999). Together they are designed to ensure that authorities are forced to set 'demanding targets for efficiency and quality improvements' (DETR, 1998, para. 4.19). However, the element of challenge is seen as the 'key to significant improvements in performance' (DETR, 1999b, para. 24), since this 'requires a fundamental rethink, asking basic questions about the needs that each service is intended to address and the method of procurement that is used' (DETR, 1999b, para. 24).

Audit and inspection

The Audit Commission has been given new powers to inspect authorities to ensure that they comply with the Best Value regime. It has established new housing and Best Value inspectorates with full-time inspectors charged with judging:

- how good services are – rated on a four-point scale from 0 (= poor) to 3 (= excellent)

- whether services have the capacity to improve in the ways required under Best Value – rated on a three-point scale ('yes', 'unlikely' and 'no') (Audit Commission, 2000, p. 10).

The quality of an authority's Best Value reviews is supposed to be an important influence on the level of external scrutiny that it receives. Inspections will mirror an authority's review programme and councils that are performing well have been promised 'lighter touch inspection'.

Inspection reports will follow a standard template covering the following issues:

1 Local people's judgements about services

2 Recommendations for improvement

3 The background to a service

4 How good are services?
   - Are the authority's aims clear and challenging?
   - Does the service meet these aims?
   - How does its performance compare to other authorities?

5   Are they going to improve?
- Does the Best Value review drive improvement?
- How good is the authority's improvement plan?
- Will the authority deliver the improvements (Audit Commission, 2000, p. 22).

Definitions of Best Value

Tensions in the Best Value framework

With legislation, guidance and inspection and audit regimes now in place what central government means by Best Value has become much clearer and more tightly defined. In some senses, the regime can be seen as the 'high-water mark' of the so-called 'New Public Management'. There is a strong emphasis upon economy and efficiency with authorities required to identify efficiency savings 'consistent with an overall target of 2% p.a. efficiency improvement for local government as a whole' (DETR, 1998). At first sight at least, the emphasis seems to be on rationing rather than choice and there is nothing in the Best Value guidance, legislation or performance indicators which encourages service providers to consider users' rights to the support that enables them to lead full and independent lives. This is, however, only part of the picture.

Whilst the Best Value regime is indeed intended to promote greater efficiency, it also places considerable emphasis on service improvement. Though initially billed simply as 'a replacement for CCT' (cf. Doyle, 1996), it has become the centrepiece of New Labour's attempt to encourage 'a radical refocusing of councils' traditional roles'. As such, it is designed to produce 'a fundamental shift of culture throughout local government' (Cm. 4014, 1998, p. 5) and, according to the White Paper, to ensure that local people get 'a better deal and a bigger say'. In the words of the then Minister for Regional and Local Government, 'At its heart Best Value seeks to reshape the relationship between local government and the electorate.' The aim is that services are no longer organised in ways which best suit providers but become increasingly 'citizen-centred'. Whilst the inspection routines, audit procedures and Best Value performance indicators (BVPIs) give the regime the appearance of rigidity, it in fact remains somewhat ambiguous. There are competing definitions of what constitutes 'Best Value' and a range of interpretations of how best to achieve it (Geddes and Martin, 2000). Questions of 'Best Value for whom' continue to loom large and there are tensions between:

- national standards and local priorities

- cost and quality of service provision

- the interests of different 'stakeholders' – users, providers, taxpayers and so forth.

CCT was abolished in part because it was seen as imposing 'bland uniformity' (Armstrong, 1997, p. 12) and the Government made it clear from the outset that 'The duty of Best Value is one that local authorities will owe to *local* people (DoE, 1997, p. 3, italics added)'. Decisions about service provision should therefore be 'taken, wherever possible, by locally informed, elected and accountable people' (DETR, 1998, para. 3.3). Central government needs 'to become less involved in the detail of local decisions' (DETR, 1998, para. 3.3) and authorities were exhorted to implement Best Value 'imaginatively and in the spirit with which it has been designed' (DETR, 1999a, para. 10). Equally, though, ministers are determined to 'drive up' the quality of services across the board and appear to have become increasingly impatient about what they perceive to be the slow pace of change. The Government has also stressed the importance of reducing spatial disparities in the costs and standards of service. Under Best Value, authorities are therefore required to set 'cost and efficiency targets over 5 years that, as a minimum, are consistent with the top 25% of authorities' (DETR, 1999b, para. 28). This in turn is leading to ever-increasing reliance on what Hoggett (1996) describes as narrow measures of 'performativity' (league tables of performance indicators, customer charters and quality standards), which, it is claimed, squeeze out innovation and local flexibility.

The trade-off between the cost and the quality of services has the potential to become a battleground for different interest groups at both national and local levels. The Treasury of course continues to stress efficiency savings. Ministers have, though, criticised the way in which CCT drove costs down at the expense of service standards – in the words of the 1997 Labour Party manifesto 'Cost counts but so does quality' (Labour Party, 1997, p. 34). The Best Value regime does not, therefore, require authorities to make individual procurement decisions purely on the basis of cost. The aim is to encourage the delivery of 'quality services at a competitive price' (Cm. 4014, para. 7.30).

At local level, the quality–cost equation is of course often viewed in different ways by different interest groups. Thus, service users, front-line staff and service managers are often seen as being the most committed to high quality services. Many trade union branches have, for example, been very suspicious of the Best Value regime, seeing it as an attempt to impose CCT style cost cutting 'through the backdoor' (Centre for Public Services, 2000; GMB, 1999). Council tax and rate payers (both individuals and businesses but especially those that do not make extensive use of local public services) on the other hand often attach much greater importance to cost-efficiency. The arrival of Best Value does nothing to obviate the need for senior officers and elected members to 'hold the ring' and to decide on the appropriate balance of costs and service standards within the tight budgets and increasingly stretching performance targets being set by Whitehall departments.

A third, and as yet largely unresolved, set of tensions concern what is meant in practice by the new duty to 'consult' and in particular how apparently competing notions of representative and participative democracy might be reconciled (Daly and Davis, 2000). The White Paper *Modernising Government* (Cm. 4310, 1999) attributes many of the current deficiencies of public services to the privileging of producer interests. There is, it argues, a need to ensure that services 'meet the needs of citizens, not the convenience of service providers' (Cm 4310, 1999, para. 20). Public participation is therefore actively promoted by the Government as an important means of achieving this shift of power and influence away from bureau professionals and front-line staff towards citizens and service users.

The 1999 Local Government Act casts the duty to consult under the Best Value regime very widely. Authorities must take account of the views of local taxpayers, service users and any other groups which have 'an interest in any area within which the authority carries out functions' (HMSO, 1999, clause 3.2). It is clear that the Government expects this to be linked to and integrated with the new powers to promote the well-being of their areas and the resulting community planning ushered in through the Local Government Act 2000. However, 'consultation' is a vague term that potentially embraces a wide range of different kinds of engagement and ministers and their officials frequently conflate very different kinds of public participation. The Local Government White Paper (Cm. 4014), for example, refers to a duty to 'consult', 'listening to local people', 'being in touch with the people', 'involving users', and strengthening 'accountability to local people' as if these are synonymous or interchangeable. As a result, central government sometimes appears to be endorsing contrasting approaches including notions of 'customer focus' derived from the US business management literature of the 1980s and early 1990s, and community empowerment and the co-production of services (Martin and Boaz, 2000).

Local implementation

These ambiguities and tensions have important implications for user involvement in service design and delivery, and the prospects for adequate resourcing of the services needed to promote independent living. In theory at least, if the national Best Value performance indicators were to take account of the objectives and benefits of promoting independent living they could prove to be a positive force for change. Similarly, if local Best Value reviews were to take a long-term perspective and employ measures of cost-effectiveness that took account of the social and economic benefits of supporting independent living, they may well conclude that there is a need to strengthen services for people with disabilities. Moreover, the statutory 'duty to consult' and the advent of Best Value performance plans open up new opportunities for service users to influence the design and delivery of services, the setting of performance targets and monitoring of service standards. If, however, national Best Value performance indicators continue to be narrowly defined (see papers by Frances Hasler and Gerry Zarb in this volume), and if Best Value reviews are primarily seen as short-term cost-cutting exercises and the duty to consult is interpreted as a requirement simply to conduct an annual survey of residents, the new regime may subvert services that support independent living. A great deal therefore depends on how the Best Value regime is interpreted and implemented at local level and, whilst it is still too early to reach definitive judgements, some indications of likely developments are provided by the authorities that piloted Best Value in advance of the legislation.

Approaches to reviews

The Best Value pilots enjoyed a greater degree of freedom than exists under the statutory regime. They piloted broad Best Value principles and their activities were not audited or inspected. The pilot initiatives therefore encompassed a wide range of different approaches to implementing the 'four Cs' and there were marked variations not just between authorities but also between individual services within authorities. However, it is possible to identify four broad emphases (Martin *et al.*, 1999). These are not mutually exclusive. Indeed, they overlap, merge and play off each other in varying combinations and to varying degrees across different services and in different authorities. However, the four broad approaches are informed by different political values and priorities, and suggest very different approaches to dealing with the tensions within the Best Value regime. In particular, they have important implications for the scope and style of user involvement in service design and delivery (see Table 3.1).

Many pilot initiatives focused upon functionally organised services such as housing management, the administration of revenues and housing benefits, leisure and community services (in particular libraries and leisure centres), residential and domiciliary care, and environmental services (e.g. refuse collection, street cleansing and waste management). These reviews were usually led by the service departments and made extensive use of service-based performance indicators to

Table 3.1 Typology of approaches to Best Value

	In-house service focus	Market focus	Issues/client group focus	Local community focus
Principal aims	Produce	Procure	Ensure appropriate provision	Engage with communities
Emphasis	Compare (standards)	Compete (voluntary competitive tendering)	Collaborate	Consult
Means	Incremental improvement in traditional welfare state	Contracting out and joint ventures	Corporate re-engineering and cultural change	Empowering communities
Structures	Strong departments and service committees	Commissioner/provider split, public–private partnerships	Corporate management team and political executive	Neighbourhood offices, area forums
Value defined in terms of	Professional standards and service-based performance indicators	Unit costs	Corporate and community priorities	Community needs and aspirations
Predominant mode of regulation	Hierarchy	Market	Internal co-ordination and external collaboration	Networks
Approach to partnership	Minimal	Public–private	Strategic partnerships	Community and inter-agency partnerships
Champions	Senior professionals, committee chairs, front-line staff	Central government, business	Senior corporate managers, leading elected members	Community groups, neighbourhood managers, ward councillors

Source: Martin (2000).

compare effectiveness and costs with those of other authorities. The aim was usually to achieve incremental improvements through more effective operational management.

The views of service users were often sought but non-users and the wider community were not usually consulted. As a result, the groups with the greatest direct stake in the service – service committees, service managers, front-line staff and service users – played a key role in defining what constitutes 'Best Value'. The extent to which review teams questioned the need for the service, or examined fundamentally different approaches to delivering it, depended on the way in which review processes were managed. Some authorities adopted highly devolved approaches, allowing individual departments and service committees to decide the timing, scope and methodology of reviews. Others gave them much less of a 'free hand' and included 'critical friends' (officers from outside the service and/or experts from other local organisations) on review teams to 'ask the difficult questions'. Some pilots (e.g. Ipswich and Southampton) set up external validation panels with members drawn from a range of organisations. On the whole, though, broader strategic issues did not loom large and contracting out to alternative service providers was often seen as a last resort to be used only in cases of continuing under-performance or gross inefficiency.

A second group of initiatives focused on market testing as the primary means of securing improvements in services such as revenues and benefits, IT provision, residential care, housing repairs, highways and park maintenance. In some cases, market testing showed in-house services to be the most efficient and effective providers. In others, authorities claim to have made significant cost savings by externalising services. In some cases, outsourcing was seen as the best means of attracting new private capital investment, particularly for school buildings, leisure centres, catering services, residential homes, information and communications systems, and housing repairs. The process of service review was generally driven by a need to reduce spending, and focused primarily on comparisons of the cost-efficiency of alternative providers. The emphasis was upon the authority as a procurer, rather than a direct provider, of services. In these cases, consultation with service users usually played only a minor role.

A third group of pilot initiatives reflected a concern with 'corporate performance', usually among pilots that have adopted a 'whole authority approach' to implementing Best Value. Many of these authorities instituted a programme of reviews that was linked explicitly to corporate, strategic objectives and was overseen directly by political executives and/or senior management teams and corporate 'Best Value officers'. Review teams were required to follow corporate Best Value protocols and to use standardised review methodologies or 'toolkits' and performance management systems, often based on the 'Business Excellence Model'. These authorities used a range of methods including attempts to improve the standard of functionally organised services, to reduce costs through market testing, and to address 'cross-cutting review' issues such as community safety, regeneration and public health through more 'holistic' services, better internal co-ordination and improved collaboration with other agencies. The common thread was, however, that definitions of 'Best Value' were closely linked to the priorities of the political and managerial leadership of the authority and were often judged largely in terms of 'managerial effectiveness'. There was often a strong emphasis on the need for corporate re-engineering and cultural change both across the authority as a whole and within individual services.

The fourth main set of pilot initiatives focused on the needs and priorities of specific communities of place, identity or interest.

Just under a fifth of the authorities that bid to participate in the pilot programme, and a quarter of those that were selected to do so, proposed to integrate the services they provided to particular wards, housing estates or neighbourhoods. A second set of community-oriented initiatives sought to address the needs of specific client groups, for example older people, pre-school children, youth and people with disabilities, in a more integrated fashion. This group of initiatives is therefore diverse. The geographical target areas, the client groups, the services involved and the extent to which authorities have been willing to cede control to communities varied considerably. However, the unifying theme was the need to 'join up' services. Review processes typically spanned a number of departments and/or agencies, and review teams usually included senior corporate officers, service managers and representatives of other local service providers. Many of these initiatives emphasised the role of 'consultation'. There was often a strong link to community planning, and many pilots adopted deliberative approaches designed to engage a range of different types of citizens in in-depth discussions about current and future priorities. The aim was sometimes to empower communities to exert greater influence over the design and delivery of services, and, in a small number of cases, local people have begun, albeit in relatively modest ways, to 'co-produce' local services.

User involvement in Best Value

The pilot initiatives, then, confirm that the scope for user involvement in Best Value will depend largely on how the new duty is interpreted and implemented at local level. A service-focused approach is likely to give users a strong voice and there are examples of pilot reviews that led to services being redesigned to provide what service users actually wanted rather than the things that professions have traditionally assumed were 'good' for them. However, service-focused reviews, whilst good at producing change at the margins, are unlikely to lead to a radical overhaul of most services. In particular, there is little scope for producing more 'joined-up' services or for the kinds of inter-organisational working that is needed to promote independent living.

A market-focused approach, though relatively unusual among the pilots, is likely to become increasingly important because of the continuing resource constraints upon authorities. Because of its emphasis on rationing rather than on users' rights and service quality, there is a danger that this approach might lead review teams to conclude that the services needed to support independent living are 'unaffordable'. The emphasis on competition and 'competitive' service providers may also disadvantage user-led groups that appear to be relatively expensive compared to private sector providers.

An approach to Best Value that emphasises corporate priorities and organisational performance carries similar risks to a market-focused approach. In particular, there is a real possibility that the focus on managerial measures of cost-effectiveness and on consulting with the citizenry as a whole will weaken the voice and diminish the influence of service users. On the other hand, the promotion of more sophisticated and in-depth deliberation about local policy options opens up new opportunities to educate service providers and the wider public about the benefits of independent living. Ultimately, the outcome of these reviews may depend on policy makers' perceptions of the levels of support among the wider community for services that promote independent living.

A community-focused approach to Best Value offers considerable scope for users with disabilities to influence service design and delivery. It is likely to promote more holistic services and there is the potential for 'user-focused' performance indicators that help to address some of the issues that are of most concern to those with disabilities. Local measures of the extent to which people feel in control of their own lives might, for example, be included in Best Value performance plans. This approach is, however, perceived to be relatively expensive and difficult choices will still need to be made between the interests of different communities of place, identity and interest.

The Best Value framework therefore embraces a range of very different approaches to, and levels of, 'consultation' depending on the definition of 'Best Value' that is adopted and which approaches to implementing the framework are seen as most appropriate in each service and each authority. In broad terms, the Best Value framework has the potential to move authorities away from customer relations towards more interactive forms of engagement involving a wider range of 'stakeholders' (Figure 3.1).

Whether it does this, though, depends on how the duty is interpreted at local level. In some cases, it was seen by pilots simply as requiring them to provide information about existing services ('communication'). Others attempted to create or to strengthen the dialogue between service providers, users and the general public ('consultation'). A few promoted the active involvement of individuals and/or communities in the design and delivery of local services ('co-production'). The boundaries between these three activities are not of course clear-cut. Indeed, many approaches (for example, 'listening events' and 'community roadshows') lend themselves to both communication and consultation, and most pilots saw both activities as important. Many used electronic information and communications and technologies such as websites, information points and CD-ROMs to provide information. There was also a marked increase in the use of residents' surveys and citizens' panels and, to a lesser

Figure 3.1 Approaches to 'consultation'

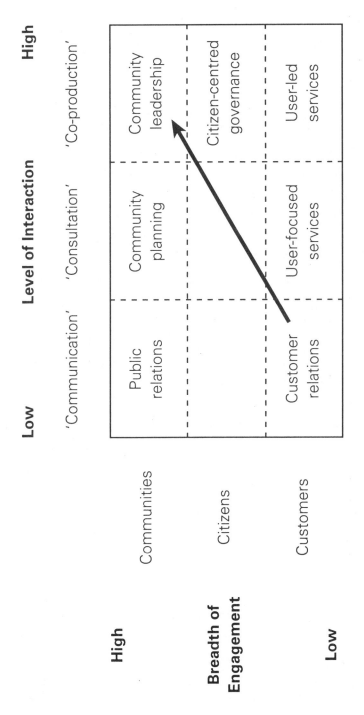

Source: Martin and Boaz (2000).

extent, citizens' juries. A number of authorities consulted local people about the sorts of information they wanted access to, the issues about which they wished to be consulted and their preferred mechanisms for consultation. A small number of authorities sought to involve local people in designing and delivering services. Leeds City Council, for example, worked closely with residents in some of the city's most deprived wards to formulate 'Best Value' strategies for addressing local needs. Manchester City Council brought community development workers, council tenants and front-line staff together to begin to review environmental and housing management services, and design strategies to tackle crime and vandalism.

Many services with a strong tradition of user involvement reported that one of the most significant impacts of the Best Value framework was that it forced them to consult future priorities and targets as well as consulting about current and past performance. Some also broadened out consultation beyond users and user representatives, making special efforts to work with non-users and specific communities of identity, place or interest – in particular so-called 'hard-to-reach groups'. Some authorities also sought to involve staff, although others are seen as having not offered the workforce meaningful opportunities to participate in Best Value reviews.

Many of the pilot reviews had a direct impact on services that support the potential for independent living. Birmingham, Brighton and Hove, Camden, Lincolnshire and others reviewed aspects of home care for the elderly. Several (including Redcar and Cleveland) reviewed occupational therapy services in year one. York is one of a number of pilots that tested out alternative methods of providing meals at home. In York, this was billed as part of a wider objective to 'help people to fulfil their wish to live at home when, because of declining health, vulnerability or disability, they need support or care' (City of York Council, 1997, p. 16). Bristol introduced a local bus service using accessible vehicles in an area from which commercial providers had withdrawn. As the direct result of a Best Value review with strong user involvement, Southampton City Council opened a new six-bed rehabilitation unit as a stepping-stone for older people leaving hospital after accident and illness. Under an initiative labelled 'every little counts', it also set aside a maximum of £1,500 per project to support small but practical improvements in the quality of life for older people – examples include the fitting of room temperature gauges under its 'Homesafe scheme' (Southampton City Council, 1999, p. 10). Cumbria's pilot involved the setting up of a new arm's-length body with responsibility for services to people with disabilities with joint funding from the county council and health authorities. This was accompanied by a wide range of methods of consulting with service users, including representation on the Learning Disability Task Groups, mechanisms to ensure wide circulation and discussion of the draft and final community care plans, and involving users in formal agreements with Councils of Voluntary Service (Cumbria County Council, 1997, pp. 5–6).

Views about the value and outcomes of these reviews have varied. In York, carers and user representatives report that their relationships with social services managers have been transformed in the course of the Best Value pilot. One leading advocacy group, for example, told us that 'the Best Value reviews have really opened social services managers' eyes to what clients want.' This has resulted in the provision of new forms of domiciliary care, which the authority had previously considered to be relatively unimportant, and greater attention to issues such as attempting to ensure continuity of carers – something which is particularly valued by some older service users. Equally, though, there were a number of cases where users and their representatives believed that their views were not taken into account sufficiently by pilot initiatives. In Birmingham, for example, proposals to close council-run elderly peoples' homes have been vociferously opposed by a residents' advocacy organisation – the Residents Action Group for the Elderly (RAGE). Amongst other complaints, RAGE reports that the social services directorate's policy for elderly care in the city 'did not outline any programme for future (as well as current) potential Service User Group involvement' (RAGE, 2000, p. 4).

Conclusions

The advent of the Best Value regime presents a range of new opportunities for user involvement, and perhaps for promoting principles and services that underpin independent living. Authorities now have a statutory duty to consult about all of the services and activities in which they are engaged. They have to make particular efforts to engage with the less vocal, less visible and perhaps less articulate members of the community. They have to involve service users not just in reviewing past performance but also in setting future targets. They are required to report progress towards meeting targets and to give an account for any failures to achieve them. The straitjacket of CCT has been removed and authorities can now think more imaginatively about ways of 'joining up' services and responding more flexibly to users' needs. There is a renewed concern to address the so-called 'cross-cutting issues', such as independent living, that pose complex service delivery and policy questions, and require co-ordinated action by several departments and/or agencies. On the downside, though, there is a real danger that reviews will focus primarily on cost savings and will not consider new or additional services that may be needed to promote independent living. There is relatively little evidence of significant new joint working between agencies and the emphasis on competition may well disadvantage user-led groups. The statutory Best Value performance indicators do not reflect support for independent living, few councils have developed their own user-focused measures, and the audit and inspection regimes have been focused largely on internal processes rather than on whether there have been real improvements in service outcomes.

It is still early days but Best Value, therefore, clearly has the potential to both offer new opportunities for and pose threats to increased user involvement and to services that promote independent living. In these circumstances, there are some important practical steps that can be taken to try to influence the development of Best Value at both national and local levels in ways that would make it more supportive of services that promote independent living.

First, there is clearly a need to argue the case with senior policy makers at national level, particularly in the Department of Health, for Best Value performance indicators that take account of the increasing acceptance within 'mainstream' social services of the importance of independent living. In particular, it will be important to develop new, outcome-focused measures that reflect most disabled people's aspiration to have a greater measure of control over their lives.

Second, there is a lot that can be done to inform and influence the implementation of Best Value at local level. It is important that local authorities are reminded of the need for 'rounded' reviews that do not just consider whether existing services are required but also whether new services are needed and how these can be provided. Local authorities also have to be encouraged and supported to develop new, more effective ways of involving users in designing and monitoring services. There are already some examples of user-controlled Best Value reviews (e.g. the review of direct payments undertaken in Wiltshire), and there is a need to disseminate these and other exemplars of good practice much more widely and proactively. Equally importantly, the development of local performance measures that reflect the needs and aspirations of people with disabilities would also be a major step forward. Very little progress has so far been made in this direction. There is, therefore, a need for indicative measures to be developed, piloted and then disseminated to authorities so that they can adopt or adapt these for use in reviews and Best Value performance plans.

Third, it will be important to monitor the ways in which Best Value reviews are implemented over the next two to three years. In particular, there is a need for accurate data on the impacts of reviews on procurement decisions and whether they discriminate against external, user-led providers. It is also important to assess whether reviews and the service improvements that follow from them lead to tangible improvements in the quality of life of people with disabilities. This might be done by keeping a comprehensive database of reviews focused on services that have a direct impact on independent living. Alternatively, it could involve tracking a sample of such reviews and evaluating the level of user involvement and users' perceptions of both the review process and the extent of improvements in service outcomes.

Note

This paper draws upon an evaluation of the Best Value pilot programme commissioned by the then Department of the Environment, Transport and the Regions (DETR) and the National Assembly for Wales. The views expressed are, however, our own and do not necessarily reflect those of the DETR, the Assembly or the pilot authorities.

Bibliography

Armstrong, H. (1997) 'In the Progress hot seat', *Progress*, Vol. 4, Spring, pp. 12–13

Audit Commission (2000) *Seeing is Believing: How the Audit Commission will Carry out Best Value Inspections in England.* London: Audit Commission

Centre for Public Services (2000) *A Socialist Agenda for Local Public Service Improvement.* Sheffield: Centre for Public Services, University of Sheffield

City of York Council (1997) *Best Value Pilot Bid.* York: City of York Council

Cm. 4014 (1998) *Modern Local Government: in Touch with the People.* London: Stationery Office

Cm. 4310 (1999) *Modernising Government.* London: Stationery Office

Cumbria County Council (1997) *Best Value in Disability and Mental Health: a Report by Cumbria County Council.* Kendal: Cumbria County Council

Daly, G. and Davis, H. (2000) 'New Labour, partnership and participation', paper presented to the ESRC New Labour and the third way public services research seminar, University of York

Davis, H. (2000) 'Every little counts towards Best Value', *Care Plan*, Vol. 6, No. 3, pp. 9–11

Department of the Environment (DoE) (1997) 'Better value for local authority services', News Release 197, 2 June

Department of the Environment, Transport and the Regions (DETR) (1997) 'Best Value framework will be simple, straightforward but challenging', News Release 299, 25 July

Department of the Environment, Transport and the Regions (DETR) (1998) *Modernising Local Government: Improving Local Services through Best Value.* London: DETR

Department of the Environment, Transport and the Regions (DETR) (1999a) *Preparing for Best Value.* London: DETR

Department of the Environment, Transport and the Regions (DETR) (1999b) *Implementing Best Value: a Consultation Paper on Draft Guidance.* London: DETR

Department of the Environment, Transport and the Regions (DETR) (1999c) *Protocol on Intervention Powers.* London: DETR

Doyle, P. (1996) 'An alternative to CCT', *Municipal Journal*, 28 June, p. 18

Geddes, M.N. and Martin, S.J. (2000) 'The policy and politics of Best Value: currents, cross-currents and undercurrents in the new regime', *Policy and Politics*, Vol. 28, No. 3, pp. 377–94

GMB (1999) *Best Ask the Workforce: GMB Shop Stewards' Experiences of Best Value in Local Government.* London: GMB

Gray, A. and Jenkins, B. (1999) 'Democratic renewal in local government: continuity and change', *Local Government Studies*, Vol. 25, No. 4, pp. 25–46

HMSO (1999) *Local Government Act 1999*. London: HMSO

Hoggett, P. (1996) 'New modes of control in the public service', *Public Administration*, Vol. 74, No. 1, pp. 9–32

Labour Party (1997) *New Labour: Because Britain Deserves Better*. London: Labour Party

Martin, S.J. (1999) 'Picking winners or piloting Best Value? An analysis of English Best Value bids', *Local Government Studies*, Vol. 25, No. 2, pp. 53–67

Martin, S.J. (2000) 'Implementing Best Value: local public services in transition', *Public Administration*, Vol. 78, No. 1, pp. 209–27

Martin, S.J. (2001) 'Best Value: new public management or new direction?', in K. Ross, S. Osborne and E. Ferlie (eds) *The New Public Management: Current Trends and Future Prospects*. London, Routledge

Martin, S.J. and Boaz, A. (2000) 'Public participation and citizen-centred local government: lessons from the Best Value and Better Government for Older People pilot programmes', *Public Money and Management*, Vol. 20, No. 2, pp. 47–54

Martin, S.J., Davis, H., Bovaird, A.G., Geddes, M., Hartley, J.F., Lewis, M., Sanderson, I. and Sapwell, P. (1999) *Improving Local Public Services: Interim Evaluation of the Best Value Pilot Programme*. London: DETR

Residents Action Group for the Elderly (RAGE) (2000) *New Homes for Old: Best Value for Whom?* Birmingham: RAGE submission to Birmingham City Council's Social Services and Health Scrutiny Committee

Southampton City Council (1999) *Better Governance and Better Value: a Better Life for Older People – First Annual Report of the Best Value Pilot*. Southampton: Southampton City Council

4 COST-EFFECTIVE SUPPORT WITHIN A FRAMEWORK OF INDEPENDENT LIVING – MEASURING COST-EFFECTIVENESS

Gerry Zarb

Introduction

A companion paper to this (from Frances Hasler and Gerry Zarb) in Part 1 of this volume outlines the principles of independent living.

The specific aim for this paper is to examine what – from the point of view of service users, disabled and older people – is good cost-effective support within a framework of independent living? What, in this context, are the strengths and weaknesses in the way that cost-effectiveness is currently defined and measured, in theory and in practice?

The first part of the paper looks in more detail at the issue of evaluating cost-effectiveness within an independent living framework. This part of the paper focuses in particular on the kinds of evaluation criteria that need to be developed in order to make a proper assessment of the costs and benefits of investing in independent living.

In the second part, we examine the key features of Best Value as they relate to independent living. This part of the paper focuses in particular on the issue of how local authorities will monitor cost-effectiveness using the Performance Assessment

Framework and how this compares with the kind of evaluation criteria implied by an independent living framework.

Measuring cost-effectiveness

Broadening out the definition of independent living to encompass the wider objectives of increasing social and economic participation has important implications for how cost-effectiveness should be defined and measured.

As we have argued elsewhere (Zarb, 1998), a key objective for future debate would be to shift the existing focus on costs towards seeing expenditure on independent living options as a form of social and economic investment. Also, that the costs and benefits of investment in independent living need to be analysed at an aggregate or macro level in order to demonstrate the overall impact of such investment in terms of both social justice and economic efficiency.

Existing approaches to this question are seriously limited by the narrow focus on individual investment decisions – as typified by the process of assessment for community care, for example. This not only precludes any meaningful discussion of overall costs and benefits but also tends to systematically exclude individuals and groups at the extremes of the cost scale for whom such investment is deemed not to be cost-effective.

A shift in focus away from individual investment decisions towards consideration of macro-level social and economic costs and benefits also implies a need to analyse the impact of investment in independent living as a process which occurs over time. This is because the costs and benefits of individual investments made at any particular point in time will obviously have longer-term effects and the pay-off – if there is one – may only be demonstrated over time. Similarly, at a macro level, the long-term impact of investment in independent living needs to be analysed in terms of the potential for bringing about changes in patterns of demand for particular forms of support and, hence, of the overall effect on public finances.

This long-term approach to investment is equally important at an individual level as it opens up the possibilities for considering how particular investments may be cost-effective over time, even if they appear expensive at the outset. Similarly, this approach would allow us to take account of the social and/or economic contribution that such investment enables people to make and, where necessary, to offset costs at one stage (in older age for example) against the benefits at an earlier stage – particularly when people are economically active.

It is also essential that any discussion of cost-effectiveness should take account of the benefits associated with alternative funding mechanisms. This would mean defining appropriate measures for the quality of outputs associated with the various support options that might be available. Such measures could then be related to both the direct and indirect costs involved. In the context of investment in independent living, the principal 'benefits' that we would need to measure are those relating to:

- how well particular personal assistance options satisfy people's needs (which could be measured by factors such as reliability, degree of choice and control, and so on)

- the wider benefits which follow from the degree of efficiency with which these needs are met (for example, by enabling people to take up employment or participate in social or cultural activities, the impact on family members, and so on).

Factors like choice, reliability, and flexibility can all – potentially at least – be assessed in an objective way. However, the biggest challenge for analysing the effectiveness of investment in independent living will be to develop appropriate measures for such factors that can be universally applied to people with a range of different needs and support arrangements.

In addition, appropriate indicators would need to be developed to assess the cost-effectiveness of investment in independent living in terms of increasing social and economic participation.

Some of these indicators could be developed at an individual level but, in order for the costs and benefits to be fully evaluated, we also need to consider some of the broader macro-level outcomes which investment in independent living might produce. These would include things like savings on social security benefits; earnings from employment; generation of tax and consumption revenues associated with increased participation in social and economic activities; the potential reduction in demand for health and social services; and the scope for reduction in dependency on informal support.

In the final part of the paper, we look at how well this framework for analysing cost-effectiveness fits in with the approach adopted in the implementation of Best Value.

Best Value

One of the main aims for the seminar was to explore our understanding of models of cost-effective service provision within a value-base of independent living that can be used practically in the development of the Best Value.

There are four key elements to the policy of Best Value as stated in the white paper, *A New Approach to Social Services Performance* (Department of Health, 1999):

"In undertaking a Fundamental Performance Review of all, or part of its social services (or indeed any other service) a local authority will need to:

- *challenge* why and how a service is being provided;

- invite *comparison* with the performance of other authorities across a range of relevant indicators (for social services these indicators are likely to be those from the Performance Assessment Framework) taking into account the views of service users and potential service providers;

- *consult* with service users, their carers, local taxpayers and the wider community in the setting of new performance targets;

- embrace *fair competition* as a means of securing efficient and effective services."

This part of the paper looks at each of these key elements of Best Value in turn and examines the implications for evaluating cost-effectiveness within an independent living framework.

Challenging assumptions about the organisation and delivery of existing services

One aspect of Best Value which, potentially at least, is most in tune with the principles of independent living is the requirement – through the drawing up of Public Service Agreements – that local authorities should be looking to challenge, or critically evaluate, existing assumptions about how support should be provided, and by whom:

"Best Value should be seen as more than just a process, it is about a cultural change, redefining perceptions of the way local services should be delivered and the way services relate to local people ... Local authorities should look at each element of their social services and ask themselves what need the service addresses, whether the service is effective in addressing the identified need and if the service could be delivered more efficiently and effectively. Fundamental performance reviews will provide an opportunity to consider the justification for existing services in this way to ensure Best Value is being achieved ... An authority will need to ensure that it is delivering the services that users and carers really want, and that services are tailored to individuals' requirements and not defined by a traditional response."

(Department of Health, 1999)

This not only opens the door to more creative kinds of support arrangements, it also implies that local authorities would need to be able to justify why they have not followed models of best practice from elsewhere. For example, if a local authority chose to run an in-house care attendant service instead of a direct payments scheme they would, presumably, need to demonstrate that this provided the same level of flexibility, choice and control as a direct payments scheme could offer. As stated in the National Priorities Guidance, when establishing local service objectives an authority would need to: 'check what other comparable authorities, and the private and voluntary sectors, are capable of achieving' (Department of Health, 1999).

In theory, this aspect of Best Value should have the effect of moving all services towards the quality levels achieved by the most successful support schemes. This does not necessarily mean that exactly the same kinds of independent living services should be implemented in all local authorities. What it does mean, however, is that all local authorities will need to be able to demonstrate that they are able to offer suitable services to support independent living.

In the context of evaluating the cost-effectiveness of independent living, this could, for example, include collecting information on the degree of choice and control that different support options offer to local people, and how these compare with best practice elsewhere. This would provide information that is both compatible with the kind of quality criteria of most importance to service users, and of direct relevance to the key outcomes which independent living is supposed to deliver. However, as we shall see from the next part of the paper, the kind of information gathering proposed for assessment of Best Value would appear to be much more limited.

Performance review and evaluating cost-effectiveness

The issue of cost-effectiveness is central to the implementation of Best Value. However, one of the problems with trying to apply this within an independent living framework is that the language of cost-effectiveness and Best Value is still often used in an over-simplified way as a proxy for cost savings. There is no mention at all, either in the policy statements or guidance notes, of the potential cost benefits of investment in independent living, or even of the longer-term outcomes of this or any other kind of support provision.

Indeed, despite the many references to the importance of measuring outcomes within the policy statements on Best Value, the actual indicators proposed for the Best Value Performance Assessment Framework are in fact heavily weighted towards inputs such as the numbers of people supported to live at home and the unit costs of various services.

As a result, although many of the overall objectives associated with Best Value are supportive of independent living principles, the approach to evaluating cost-effectiveness within the Best Value performance assessment framework appears much more limited in scope (see Box 4.1)

Box 4.1 The proposed National Best Value Performance Indicators

(i)   National priorities and strategic objectives
A1   Stability of placements of children looked after
A2   Educational qualifications of children looked after
A3   Re-registrations on the Child Protection Register
A4   Employment, education and training for care leavers
A5   Emergency admissions for older people [INTERFACE]
A6   Emergency psychiatric readmissions [INTERFACE]

(ii)   Cost and efficiency
B7   Unit costs of children's residential care
B8   Unit costs of foster care
B9   Unit costs of residential and nursing care for older people
B10   Unit costs of residential and nursing care for people with learning disabilities
B11   Unit costs of residential care for people with mental illness
B12   Unit costs of residential care for people with physical disabilities
B13   Unit costs of home care for adults

(iii)   Effectiveness of service delivery and outcomes
C14   Long-term stability of placements for children looked after
C15   Cautions and convictions for children looked after
C16   Health of children looked after

C17 Reviews of child protection cases
C18 Duration on the Child Protection Register
C19 Service mix indicator for children's services
C20 Children looked after excluded from school
C21 Inspection of children's homes
C22 Supported admissions of older people to residential/ nursing care
C23 Supported admissions of adults aged 18–64 to residential/nursing care
C24 Intensive home care
C25 Adults with physical disabilities helped to live at home
C26 Adults with learning disabilities helped to live at home
C27 Adults with mental health problems helped to live at home
C28 Older people (aged 65 or over) helped to live at home
C29 Avoidable harm for adults (suicide)
C30 Avoidable harm for adults (falls and hypothermia)
C31 Inspection of adult residential care

(iv)   Quality of services for users and carers
D32 Children looked after under agreed short-term placements
D33 Allocation of single rooms
D34 Percentage of items of equipment costing less than £1,000 delivered within three weeks
D35 Percentage of people receiving a statement of their needs and how they will be met
D36 Clients receiving a review
D37 Delayed discharge [INTERFACE]
D38 Discharge from hospital [INTERFACE]
D39 Number of nights respite care provided/funded
D40 Day care for older people
D41 Carer assessments
D42 Waiting times for care packages

(v) Fair access
E43 Spending on children in need
E44 Proportion of children looked after
E45 Home care coverage
E46 Day care for adults (aged 18–64)

Note: INTERFACE denotes an indicator of performance at the NHS/social care boundary common to both the social services and health service Performance Assessment Frameworks.

Source: Department of Health (1999).

There would appear to be two main reasons for this.

First, as highlighted in the Department of Health funded research on outcomes of community care, there are a number of potential obstacles to the introduction of systems for collecting outcome and cost-effectiveness information. These include: professional resistance to specifying objectives; scepticism about the purpose intended; conceptual difficulties; overload of change and pressure to collect information; and inadequate IT systems (Qureshi and Nocon, 1995).

Local authority managers interviewed during the research, for example, felt that practical tools that were less demanding than research measures were required, and that data collection requirements should fit in with what people were doing already (Nocon *et al.*, 1996). While it is understandable that social services practitioners might be reluctant to take on large amounts of additional information gathering, it is difficult to see how the kind of analysis we have suggested could be successfully completed as long as this remains the stock response.

However, expecting social services themselves to take the lead on this – as implied by the policy of Best Value – is probably unrealistic. Although they will be expected to carry out local surveys on basic Best Value criteria, such as user satisfaction with local services, these are intended to provide only fairly 'low-level' management information. It is unlikely therefore that information from local surveys would provide the level of detail required for tracking some of the broader and longer-term outcomes of investing in independent living. Rather, it would be more appropriate for the Department of Health (through the Social Services Inspectorate) to either carry out, or commission, such research directly.

Second, although the Performance Assessment Framework does include a large number of indicators relating to Best Value and cost-effectiveness, many of these are to be based on existing statistical returns rather than on new criteria specifically formulated for the task. Given the pressures on local authority information systems noted earlier, it is not altogether surprising that this approach has been adopted. Nevertheless, it does raise doubts about whether or not such indicators could even begin to provide the kind of information that would be needed for a thorough and rigorous evaluation of the cost-effectiveness of independent living along the lines we have suggested.

Indeed, in some cases, it is difficult to see how the proposed indicators that do supposedly relate to independent living bear any relation to the kind of user-focused quality criteria discussed earlier (see Chapter 1 – 'Cost-effective support within a framework of independent living'). The Department of Health proposes to introduce a set of 46 National Social Services Performance Indicators (PIs), to be used in conjunction with the Best Value Performance Assessment Framework. These PIs are intended 'to form the basis of a shared understanding of performance issues'. There are five specific PIs proposed for assessing performance against the National Objective: 'To promote the independence of adults assessed as needing social care support arranged by the local authority, respecting their dignity and furthering their social and economic participation.' These are:

D33   Allocation of single rooms

C25   Adults with physical disabilities helped to live at home

C26   Adults with learning disabilities helped to live at home

C27   Adults with mental health problems helped to live at home

E46   Day care for adults (aged 18-64) (Department of Health, 1999).

It really is quite difficult to see exactly on whose understanding of independent living these indicators are based. Other than a very crude indication of the relative priority given to community and residential based support, these bear very little similarity to any of the different aspects of independent living discussed in this paper. Indeed, there appears to be only a very tenuous link with the stated National Objective itself. Although the issue of 'dignity' is touched on in the indicator relating to the allocation of private rooms for people in residential homes, there is nothing that measures either the quality of support provided in different settings or, most importantly, the actual outcomes in terms of promoting social and economic participation. So, even allowing for the fact that these indicators will be supplemented by information from local and national surveys, it seems that the evaluation framework for Best Value still falls some way short of the ideals portrayed in the National Objectives that the policy is intended to deliver.

Another significant restriction on analysing the cost-effectiveness of independent living within the existing Best Value framework is the timescale over which local authorities are required to monitor performance towards meeting National Objectives such as the promotion of independent living. The proposed Performance Assessment Framework requires local authorities to monitor performance within a five-year cycle. Although there is some local discretion regarding the timing of particular information-gathering exercises within a five-year cycle, there is also a requirement that all information is collected within 'a reasonable period timescale' (Department of Health, 1999).

As suggested earlier, a proper evaluation of the costs and benefits of investing in independent living would require tracking outcomes over a significant timeframe (i.e. years rather than months) so that the full range of costs and benefits can be assessed. While it may be impractical to expect that this could be carried out within the Best Value Performance Assessment Framework, this does not necessarily lessen the significance of this kind of analysis to the development of Best Value policy itself. Indeed, it could be argued that, without access to this kind of information, it would be very difficult to reliably assess the true impact of Best Value on the lives of local communities. Again, what would be left is essentially a much weaker set of proxy indicators relating to service inputs and costs rather than long-term outcomes.

Another potential limitation on the use of standardised Best Value performance indicators is that there are still quite wide local and regional variations in both the policy and practice of independent living. As mentioned earlier, implementation of Best Value means that local authorities will be expected to compare their performance with others using a range of performance indicators (PIs). The idea behind such comparison is not only to check on progress towards meeting the National Objectives, but also to highlight areas of good practice which, according to the Department of Health (1999), 'should help authorities identify which other authorities may be able to help them to improve their own performance'.

However, one potential problem with applying this approach to independent living is finding suitable points of comparison, particularly in authorities where there is no tradition of supporting independent living. Contrasting an independent living scheme, where people commission and control their own support, with, say, a home care scheme, where support is commissioned and controlled by others, will not necessarily provide very meaningful comparisons.

Consultation and user involvement

Consultation and user involvement are also supposed to be central to the implementation of Best Value. As stated in the Guidance documents for local authorities:

> "Meaningful consultation can make services more responsive and can also increase public confidence in those services. In developing targets for the cost and quality of services to deliver Best Value, local authorities will be expected to consult widely with the local community."
>
> (Department of Health, 1999)

However, although the importance of user involvement in setting Best Value targets is recognised, the decision on how to define cost-effectiveness still largely rests with central government and professional organisations. This means that there is a potentially critical contradiction at the heart of the Best Value policy. As we have already seen, this tends to result in the production of performance indicators that seem to bear very little resemblance to the kind of quality criteria that are most important to disabled people themselves.

This can be particularly limiting in the context of trying to apply what are – essentially – professionally defined performance indicators to independent living. Specifically, there is a potential danger attached to making quality indicators too systematic, too formal, and – as a result – too far removed from the highly individual and flexible nature of support systems framed by the principles of independent living.

This is not to say that quality assurance has no place in the context of independent living. Clearly, the drive to improve the quality of support systems across the board is in everyone's interests. But it does, perhaps, imply the need for a different kind of quality assurance – one that is based firmly on the needs and preferences of individuals. Attempting to force individual needs and preferences into a quality assurance framework based on some kind of universal standards (assuming these could ever be agreed in the first place) surely has the potential to limit the very flexibility at the heart of independent living.

Competition and competitive tendering

The final element of Best Value is the requirement for local authorities to use competition and competitive tendering when they are commissioning services:

"Local authorities should seek to provide services of a quality and cost that bear comparison with the best – the best provided by other local authorities and by the private and voluntary sectors. Embracing fair competition will provide authorities with a test of whether their services deliver Best Value for local people. Authorities should be able to demonstrate how the choices they make about the provision of services deliver Best Value and optimum outcomes for users and carers ... An open approach to competition with external providers based on partnership, not confrontation, will be key to securing continuous improvements in the quality and cost of social services."

(Department of Health, 1999)

Again, although there is nothing wrong with this as a general principle, there are doubts about whether it can be applied in a straightforward way to user-led support services, such as those offered by Centres for Independent Living. Further, the process of reviewing and tendering contracts implied in Best Value can easily lose sight of the focus on partnership and collaboration, and become simply about finding the cheapest provider.

This can be illustrated by a recent example in one London borough concerning the commissioning of a direct payments support service. The long-established, innovative and respected personal assistance support scheme in the borough was not awarded the contract even though they are recognised nationally as one of the leaders in this field. Another organisation, not based in the borough, was chosen instead. As tender documents and the tender process are confidential, it is not possible to say for certain how this decision was arrived at. What we do know for sure, however, is that the existing local scheme has been providing a higher level of training and peer support than the new organisation has been providing in other boroughs where it operates. It is also known that the successful bid was cheaper than that submitted by the existing local organisation.

In another recent example from a different local authority, a user-led organisation was excluded from tendering to run a support scheme. One of the main reasons given for this decision was that it was too small to take on a contract of this size. In the event, the contract was subsequently awarded to a traditional non-user-led organisation, which was considered to have more extensive resources.

The importance of these examples to the debate about cost-effectiveness in the context of Best Value is twofold. First, there is the question of who specifies what constitutes 'value'. How important are users' views when weighed against other interests? Second, there are process issues to consider: in particular, the need to take account of how the formal contracting process might be adapted to incorporate the creative, user-led ethos of independent living.

Conclusions

The main conclusion that can be drawn from this paper is that there is a large gap between the concept of independent living and the policy of Best Value.

Although at least some of the key principles of independent living are recognised within the national objectives for modernising social services, it is difficult to see how these have been translated into the various indicators that are to be used to evaluate cost-effectiveness within the Best Value framework. Indeed, it is often difficult to see how some of these indicators relate to the stated policy objectives that they are supposed to be assessing. At best, many of them are simply very loosely defined proxies that are, perhaps, unlikely to produce very much meaningful information about cost-effectiveness.

In particular, the performance indicators relating specifically to the objectives of promoting independent living and increasing social and economic participation seem to bear very little relation to the kind of outcomes which we would normally associate with independent living. Similarly, none of the proposed Best Value performance indicators reflect any of the quality criteria – such as choice and control, reliability or flexibility – which are known to be of most importance to disabled people themselves. Further, although some of the performance indicators will be supplemented by survey data on issues such as user satisfaction, it is expected that this kind of information will be fairly limited.

More generally, it is clear that the majority of the various performance indicators proposed for the evaluation of Best Value are not really focused on outcomes at all. Rather, the main focus appears to be on inputs and unit costs, which are the chief components of existing social services management information systems. It appears therefore that – in practice – cost-effectiveness within the Best Value framework is being used as an over-simplified proxy for cost savings.

Most importantly, there is no consideration at all of the potential cost benefits of investment in independent living, or the broader impact on economic and public welfare systems.

In conclusion, although it is clearly desirable to evaluate the cost-effectiveness of independent living and other support options, it is difficult to see how this could be successfully achieved within the existing Best Value Performance Assessment Framework. Indeed, there is such a limited amount of common ground between the concepts of independent living and Best Value that it is difficult even to identify a suitable starting point for modifying the existing framework. Rather, it is difficult to avoid the conclusion that the best way forward would be to scrap the current Best Value Performance Assessment Framework altogether and replace it with a completely new set of outcome and cost-effectiveness criteria more in keeping with the principles of independent living.

Bibliography

Barnes, C. (1997) *Older People's Perceptions of Direct Payments and Self Operated Support Schemes*. Leeds: University of Leeds

Department of Health (1998) *Modernising Social Services*. London: Stationery Office

Department of Health (1999) *A New Approach to Social Services Performance*. London: Stationery Office

Nocon, A. and Qureshi, H. (1996) *Outcomes of Community Care for Service Users and Carers: a Social Services Perspective*. Buckingham: Open University Press

Nocon, A., Qureshi, H. and Thornton, P. (1996) *The Perspectives of Users and Carers' Organisations*. Outcomes in Community Care Practice Series No. 4. York: Social Policy Research Unit, University of York

Qureshi, H. and Nocon, A. (1995) *Key Issues in Outcome Measurement for Practice*. Outcomes in Community Care Practice Series No. 1. York: Social Policy Research Unit, University of York

Zarb, G. (1998) 'What price independence?', in M. Turner (ed.) *Facing our Futures*. London: NCIL

Zarb, G. and Oliver, M. (1993) *Ageing with a Disability: What do they Expect after all these Years?* London, University of Greenwich

Zarb, G. and Nadash, P. (1994) *Cashing in on Independence: Comparing the Costs and Benefits of Cash and Services*. Derby: BCODP/PSI

DISCUSSION

The group discussed some of the issues surrounding the present implementation of Best Value. It was seen as an important area where concepts of cost-effectiveness and independent living needed to be applied. But, from the comments made in the discussion, it was doubtful that Best Value in its present development could add to ideas of cost-effectiveness and independent living. The current stage of development of performance indicators, for example, was vague and unsatisfactory. In social care and disability, some of the performance indicators were still about volumes of service delivery, based on formulaic ideas of support. Achieving the performance may actually act completely against ideas of independent living. In terms of national standard setting, they were problematic too, in that the present arrangements gave considerable scope for local autonomy. The paradox was evident in government statements, which *both* devolved responsibility to the local level *and* looked to achieve national government's objectives of squeezing out problem areas and pursuing 'top-down' definitions of quality.

Best Value was framed in concepts of 'effectiveness', 'utility' and 'consequence' (which were developed later in the discussion). These concepts were crucial for disabled people. If the focus was on an individual at one stage in their life where costs were particularly high, that might exclude them (and mean that 'independent living' principles were applied only to people with lower support needs). It might also unfairly exclude the societal and financial contributions that they had made in earlier years. There was a need for a view which both valued the individual throughout their life and which recognised that independent living could be a pragmatic preventive strategy in the longer term.

In summary, the time was ripe to address ideas of cost-effectiveness in current policy and practice. Best Value presented one route to addressing this, though that process should be regarded as being at the start, not at the end, of the journey.

PART 3

TOWARDS A MODEL OF COST-EFFECTIVENESS AND INDEPENDENT LIVING

5 THE APPLICATION OF HEALTH ECONOMIC TECHNIQUES TO SOCIAL CARE

Sarah Byford

Introduction

Economics and health economics

Economics is an important input into many aspects of public policy, including health care, agriculture, the environment and overseas development. In recent years, the growth in health economics has been particularly acute with economists contributing to many areas of health policy, including the structure and finance of the National Health Service (NHS), the evaluation of new treatments, the measurement of quality of life and the role of government regulation. Although economic evaluation in the social care field is in its infancy, the demand for such analysis is growing and appropriate economic techniques are needed. This paper explores the methods of economic evaluation developed in the health care field and discusses the application of these techniques to social care research.

Health economics is, quite simply, the application of economic principles to issues of health and health care. The definition of economics, however, is not so simple. *The Penguin Dictionary of Economics* defines the subject as a 'science concerned with those aspects of social behaviour, and those institutions, which are involved in the use of scarce resources to produce and distribute goods and services in the satisfaction of human wants' (Bannock *et al.*, 1984). Although accurate, this definition provides the non-economist with little information on which to build an understanding. Ray Robinson, in a series of articles on economic evaluation, provides a clearer picture stating that: 'The central concern of economics is how to use available resources best when these resources are insufficient to meet total needs' (Robinson, 1993a).

Two important economic issues are highlighted by Robinson's definition. First, resources available to society are limited and, second, demands on those resources are not. This conflict can be clearly demonstrated in the NHS. Technological advances in health care have resulted in rising costs, due in part to their relative expense but also due to changing expectations in the population. The ability to treat more and more medical conditions has brought about a corresponding increase in the number of conditions for which people expect to receive treatment. Society, however, is prepared to devote only a limited proportion of its scarce resources to health care and inevitably decisions of who should be treated and how have to be made. The same is true of social care. Budget limitations mean that social care cannot be provided to all those in need. Instead, priorities must be set and decisions made about who receives care and the quantity of care they should receive. Economics is concerned with making these priority-setting decisions in an explicit and rational manner.

Welfare economics

To set priorities in any area where resources are limited, two variables must be considered: costs and benefits. A common misconception is the view that economists are interested wholly or primarily in costs. The evaluation of costs alone, however, is meaningless. Economics is the study of welfare or well-being and the viewpoint taken is societal. Economists are thus concerned with the effect of an action on the well-being of the whole of society, not just on the individuals directly involved. The provision of residential services for people who misuse drugs, for example, does not impact only on service users, but will also affect families and friends, health and social services, the criminal justice sector and the general public. These effects may be negative (costs) or positive (benefits) and the aim is to ensure that total benefits to society outweigh total costs, resulting in an overall improvement in society's total well-being. This aim is the central component of welfare economics – the theoretical framework on which economic evaluation is based (Drummond et al., 1999).

The economist's definition of cost (opportunity cost) reflects this concern for society's well-being. By choosing to devote resources to one area of social care, society is, because total resources are limited, forgoing the benefits that would have arisen had those resources been used to fund an alternative social service. If a local authority spent its entire budget on services for children, for example, society would miss out on the benefits that would have arisen from services for adults. Cost, therefore, does not relate only to the price you pay for a service but also to the benefits (or opportunities) that are lost by not directing those resources to their next best alternative use. Social care professionals would like to provide the best care available to all users, regardless of cost, but this ignores the fact that, with limited resources, a decision to care for one individual means that those resources are being denied to others. For this reason, it is essential that resources are allocated to those individuals who can benefit from them the most.

Efficiency

Using information on costs and benefits, the economist's criterion for deciding upon a desirable allocation of resources is efficiency. In order to provide good quality care to the maximum possible number of patients, decision makers must ensure that resources are used efficiently. Goods and services must be produced at minimum cost (technical efficiency) and resources must be allocated so as to satisfy the most highly valued wants or needs (allocative efficiency) (McGuire *et al.*, 1992). To ensure efficiency in the allocation of resources, it is necessary for social care interventions and policy changes to be evaluated to establish both their effectiveness and cost-effectiveness.

Methods of economic evaluation

In health economics, five main methods of economic evaluation are used to compare the efficiency of alternative health care interventions: cost-minimisation analysis (CMA), cost-effectiveness analysis (CEA), cost consequences analysis (CCA), cost-utility analysis (CUA) and cost-benefit analysis (CBA). These methods of evaluation all involve the identification, measurement and comparison of all relevant costs and benefits, and they all measure costs in monetary terms. They differ, however, in their approach to measuring the benefits, or outcomes, of interventions under examination and the method chosen will depend on the type of study to be undertaken (Drummond *et al.*, 1999).

Cost-minimisation analysis

CMA is the simplest form of economic evaluation that can be used when there is good evidence (from scientific research) to suggest that the interventions under consideration are equally effective. Given equal outcomes, the evaluation involves the comparison of costs alone, to determine the least cost alternative (Robinson, 1993b). Where outcomes are expected to vary, alternative methods of economic evaluation should be employed.

Cost-effectiveness analysis

CEA is the most commonly adopted approach to economic evaluation in health care and involves the measurement of benefits in 'natural' or 'condition-specific' units such as level of blood pressure, life years gained or level of depression (Robinson, 1993c). The benefits of two or more interventions are combined with their respective costs to provide a measure of cost-effectiveness. Where one intervention is found to dominate the others (i.e. is more effective and less costly, more effective and equally costly, or equally effective and less costly), a formal cost-effectiveness analysis is not essential. However, where one intervention is found to produce greater benefit for greater cost, an incremental cost-effectiveness analysis is required (Drummond *et al.*, 1999). Incremental analysis involves the calculation of the ratio of additional benefits to additional costs produced by one intervention in comparison to another. This cost-effectiveness ratio can then be compared to other interventions employing the same measure of effect and preference should be given to those with the lowest incremental cost-effectiveness ratio.

The use of natural units of outcome makes CEA easily transferable into social care research, where natural units would include such things as measures of disability or social exclusion. CEA does have its weaknesses, however.

First, it is impossible to make comparisons across a diverse spectrum of interventions competing for a share of a finite budget. Social care is extremely varied and the aims and outcomes of

91

services provided will differ greatly. Comparisons of cost-effectiveness using natural units can only be made between interventions whose outcomes can be measured on the same scale. Thus, CEA can be used to support funding decisions between two competing schemes for reducing homelessness, but it cannot determine whether the same money would be better spent on a scheme to support single parents.

Second, it is difficult to capture all possible effects of an intervention on a single condition-specific outcome scale. Social care services will often influence many areas of an individual's life, but combining costs with multi-dimensional outcomes measured on a number of different scales makes interpretation difficult, particularly if improvements are seen on some scales but not others. To illustrate, a scheme that provides home adaptations for the promotion of independent living for disabled people may have an impact on psychological, social and family functioning, as well as activities of daily living. All these areas can be measured in natural units but a CEA can only be carried out with one outcome scale. Under such circumstances, a 'primary' outcome measure must be selected, requiring some judgement to be made about the relative value of the alternative outcome measures.

Cost consequences analysis

CCA is one method that has been employed to overcome the problem of capturing all relevant consequences within a CEA. CCA simply involves the presentation of a range of outcome measures alongside the costs. No attempt is made to formally combine costs with benefits and the decision maker is left to form his or her own opinion regarding the relative importance of the alternative outcome scales presented (Drummond *et al.*, 1999). Although CCA is limited by the inability to rank interventions in terms of cost-effectiveness, in the absence of adequate measures capable of capturing all the consequences of a particular intervention, it is likely to be a useful tool for social care research. The presentation of all costs and consequences can greatly enhance the understanding gained from a CEA and, thus, CCA should be encouraged even when a primary outcome measure has been selected and a CEA carried out.

Cost utility analysis

An alternative solution to multiple outcomes is to condense them into one generic measure, which is the approach adopted by CUA, a specific form of CEA. As with CEA, a cost-effectiveness ratio can be calculated, but outcomes are measured in terms of utility (level of satisfaction, pleasure, well-being, quality of life, etc.) (Robinson, 1993d). One example of a utility-based measure is the quality adjusted life year (QALY) (Drummond et al., 1999; Loomes and McKenzie, 1989). The calculation of QALYs involves the use of quality adjustment weights (or utilities) for different outcome states. There are a number of different methods of valuing these states and a number of potential respondents, such as users, the general public or professionals (McGuire et al., 1992). Once generated, the utility weights are multiplied by the time spent in each state and then summed to provide the number of quality adjusted life years, thereby incorporating the effects of an intervention on both the quantity and quality of life. The results are expressed in terms of the incremental cost per QALY gained from undertaking a particular intervention, providing a common measure of output that allows comparisons to be made between any number of diverse interventions. Resources should then be directed towards those interventions that involve the lowest cost per QALY ratio.

The theory behind utility measures is attractive and their importance should not be dismissed, but a number of weaknesses exist that may limit the usefulness of CUA within the field of social care, at least in the short term. Conceptually, the idea of condensing the benefits of a scheme for urban regeneration, for example, into a single outcome measure can be hard to swallow. In addition, utility scales have been criticised for the methodology employed, for their lack of sensitivity to change and for ignoring equity considerations (Drummond, 1991; Loomes and McKenzie, 1989; Williams and Kind, 1992). As research continues to improve on these problems, however, the usefulness of utility scales will grow.

Perhaps the main obstacle to the use of CUA in social care is the lack of utility scales appropriate to the field. Although a significant quantity of research has been carried out into the development of utility scales for use in health economics, these measures tend to be health related and may not be broad enough to capture the full impact of social care policies. The development of appropriate generic measures is needed and much of the methodological literature relating to the valuation of health-related quality of life could be drawn on for this purpose.

Cost-benefit analysis

CBA requires both costs and benefits to be valued in monetary units. It thus becomes possible to compare the costs with the benefits of an individual project to see which are greater, without the need for a comparator (Robinson, 1993e). To improve the allocation of resources, an intervention should be adopted if the benefits exceed the costs and vice versa. This approach, like CUA, allows the comparison of any number of diverse interventions since the benefits are always measured in terms of money. In addition, it is possible to compare interventions across sectors, such as health care, education or defence. The problem, however, is how to value benefits in monetary terms. How do you decide how much an increase in the length of a person's life is worth? How do you put a monetary value on freedom from abuse or avoidance of homelessness? Methods do exist to answer questions like these, such as willingness to pay, revealed preferences or human capital approaches (Drummond *et al.*, 1999), but they are not problem-free, thus CBA in health care is relatively rare and likely to be so in social care research.

Evaluation of costs

Types of costs

All the methods of economic evaluation described above require the identification and measurement of all costs relevant to the interventions under investigation (Drummond *et al.*, 1999). Costs can be split into two main categories:

- *direct costs*, which include the cost of the interventions and any costs incurred as a result of the interventions, such as travel to and from services or child care arrangements

- *indirect costs*, which refer to productivity losses that result from the need to take time off work.

The need to include all relevant direct costs is not disputed in health economics. The inclusion of indirect costs, however, is debated because of criticisms of the valuation methods used. Indirect costs are often valued on the basis of an individual's gross earnings, to reflect the actual loss of productivity that results from premature death or disability, or the gains that result from health improvements. This 'human capital' approach, however, implicitly values the time of children, housewives, pensioners and the unemployed at zero. In addition, it ignores the fact that workers absent for short periods of time can often 'catch up' on their return or their work can be covered by other staff members. For longer periods of absence, the existence of unemployment allows workers to be replaced at little cost. For these reasons, attention has turned to the friction cost method of calculation, which attempts to account for the level of scarcity in the labour market (Koopmanschap and Rutten, 1996).

A number of authors have suggested that indirect costs should be excluded from economic evaluations unless inclusion is likely to have a large impact on the results of a study (Luce and Elixhauser, 1990). Many areas of social care, however, are directly concerned with a person's ability to work, thus the exclusion of indirect costs should be considered carefully. Examples include interventions that are aimed at improving the education or employment status of individuals, such as training schemes or supported workshops, and services aimed at promoting independent living.

Perspective

The identification of costs relevant to an individual study will depend, to a large extent, on the perspective of the study. Economic evaluations in health care often take the perspective of the health service alone. Economics, however, is concerned with the impact of an action on the well-being of the whole of society, not just on the individuals or organisations directly involved and the exclusion of certain sectors may alter the conclusions of a study (Byford and Raftery, 1998). Narrow perspectives may result in a sub-optimal allocation of resources and a corresponding loss in societal well-being, and this risk will be particularly acute in areas of care which involve multiple-agencies, as is often the case in social care.

An evaluation of intensive case management for people suffering from a mental illness, for example, may appear to be cost-ineffective from the perspective of the NHS alone. Intensive case management, involving reduced case load sizes, is a more expensive model of care than standard case management since a greater number of staff are required to support the same number of people. This extra expenditure may not be justified by the additional benefits gained, such as improved social functioning and quality of life, or costs saved, such as reduced reliance on hospital services. If the perspective was widened to include all agencies, however, we may discover that intensive support reduces costs further by diminishing reliance on services provided elsewhere, such as social services, voluntary sector services or supported accommodation. Widening the perspective further to include the impact on families may reveal additional cost savings or gains in well-being, such as reductions in informal care needs and improvements in the quality of life of families. In addition, the inclusion of indirect costs may uncover a positive impact on the ability of patients to work and thus productivity losses will be reduced. When all perspectives are included, the conclusion of a study may be very different from the conclusion derived from a limited perspective.

No mention has been made so far of social security benefits, known to economists as transfer payments. This is because transfer payments, unlike the costs discussed above, are payments that are not made in return for some productive service, but are methods of redistributing wealth within a society (Drummond et al., 1999). With a societal perspective, transfer payments should be excluded from economic analyses because they do not involve either a cost or a benefit to society as a whole. However, with a narrower perspective, such as that of all government-funded agencies, social security benefits may be of interest.

Service-use data

Once the perspective of a study has been decided upon, the next step is to design appropriate methods of collecting service-use information. Before costs can be calculated, all relevant services used by individuals over the period of the study must be recorded and a number of methods exist, including service-use questionnaires, service-use diaries or searches of case notes.

Service-use questionnaires can be self-reported or completed by researchers at interview and the choice will often depend on the practicality of carrying out interviews and the complexity of the questionnaire. Where interviews are already planned for the collection of outcome data and where service-use questionnaires are particularly long or complex, the preference would be for completion during interview. Self-report may be preferable, however, when interview time is limited or unavailable, but only for short and simple questionnaires. A number of service-use questionnaires have been designed for use within health economic evaluations and, of more relevance to social care research, mental health service evaluations, such as the Client Service Receipt Interview (Beecham and Knapp, 1992). Such questionnaires often need to be adapted for the study of concern, as some services may be used only within specific areas of health or social care.

The disadvantage of questionnaires is the need to rely on the memory of interviewees over what can be a significant number of months. Service-use diaries are one method of improving recall and simply involve asking participants to record their use of services prospectively over the period of a study. An alternative method of enhancing accuracy is to collect information directly from case notes. For a more detailed elaboration of data collection methods, see Mauskopf *et al.* (1996) and Moser and Kalton (1993).

Unit cost data

The total cost of caring for each individual over the period of an evaluation is calculated by multiplying service-use data by appropriate unit costs. In many instances, local service providers will be able to supply unit cost information or the raw data needed to calculate the costs directly. For further information on direct cost estimation, see Netten and Beecham (1993), Beecham (1995) or Drummond *et al.* (1999). Where local data is unavailable, or for services that add little to the total cost of care, it is possible to find many national or regional unit costs in the published literature. Examples include *Unit Costs of Health and Social Care* (Netten *et al.*, 1999), *Personal Social Services Statistics* (CIPFA, 1999) and *The Health Service Financial Database* (CIPFA, 1998).

Evaluation of outcomes

Since the method of economic evaluation selected is influenced by the measure of effectiveness employed, and vice versa, careful thought should be given to the choice of outcome scales. Economics is concerned with maximising well-being, so, ideally, outcome measures should reflect this goal by measuring the impact of an intervention on the overall well-being of individuals. In practice, measures of effectiveness selected are often inadequate for this purpose. Condition-specific scales, such as pain or depression level, are commonly used, rather than measures that capture the full range of effects an intervention may have on a person's well-being. In addition, intermediate measures may be selected, such as days in residential care avoided, rather than measures of final outcome.

Condition-specific and generic outcome measures

In health care, condition- or disease-specific scales aim to measure, in natural units, the outcomes of treatment that are specific to a particular disease. They are mainly ordinal measures that are used to classify a disease and monitor its progression over time. Similar condition-specific scales, designed with a particular client group or need in mind, are used in social care research, such as measures of social functioning or mobility. These scales are generally sensitive to changes in the condition under investigation and can be used to carry out a CEA. They are limited, however, by their inability to capture all the potential impacts of an intervention and the impossibility of comparing diverse interventions, as discussed above (Drummond, 1991). Generic measures, used in CUA, are designed to measure all aspects of the quality of a person's life and, therefore, can be more widely applied than condition-specific scales and compared more broadly. Although some of the weaknesses of generic scales have been discussed, improving an individual's quality of life is central to both social care and health care, and efforts to measure such well-being should be encouraged.

Intermediate and final outcome measures

The use of intermediate or process measures of outcome is a further limiting factor of many studies (Drummond *et al.*, 1999). An evaluation of early hospital discharge schemes for older people, for example, may be concerned primarily with enabling people to return home to a more independent lifestyle. Return home, however, and similar outcome measures, such as days of homelessness avoided or admissions to local authority care avoided, are intermediate measures that involve implicit assumptions about what is and what isn't a 'good' outcome.

Although a majority of older people may highly value the ability to live in their own homes, others, perhaps those who have few relatives to care for them or a greater fear of isolation, may prefer to remain within an institutional environment. Similarly, admission to local authority care or accommodation for some young people may be preferable to remaining at home. More appropriate outcome measures would be those that measure final outcomes, such as satisfaction or quality of life. For more detailed information on outcome measurement in economic evaluation, see Kind (1988) and Drummond (1991).

Design of economic evaluations

Economic evaluations are quantitative in nature, and the design of trials capable of producing good quantitative evidence of both effectiveness and cost may differ from designs used more commonly in social care research, such as those that are primarily qualitative.

Choice of comparator

The first step in the design of an economic evaluation is the selection of appropriate comparators, as this can have significant implications for the results. To assess the true cost-effectiveness, the appropriate comparator should be the next best alternative, i.e. the alternative that demonstrates the opportunity cost of not undertaking the new intervention (Drummond *et al.*, 1999; Kavanagh and Stewart, 1995). Identification of this alternative, however, is not always obvious. At the very least, new interventions should be compared to current best practice, but, where a number of possible alternatives exist, it may be necessary to include a range of comparators, for example the most widely used practice as well as local practice, where these differ.

Internal and external validity

The scientific integrity of a quantitative evaluation depends upon the validity of the trial (Drummond *et al.*, 1999; Moser and Kalton, 1993). Internal validity is achieved if observed differences in outcome are due only to the difference in intervention received. The presence of confounding factors (other factors that influence the outcome of a trial) reduces the internal validity of a trial and efforts must be made to minimise such biases. Typically, trials can be confounded when the two groups of participants differ in some fundamental way. Where professionals involved in the care of participants, for example, are responsible for their allocation, there is a natural tendency to allocate individuals to the intervention that is felt to be most appropriate to their needs. The result, however, may be an excess of more severe cases in one group and the differences in outcome observed could thus be a result of the initial differences in severity and not a result of the interventions received. Trials can also be confounded when the interventions under investigation are not under the control of the researchers, for example when the comparison or control group has access to the alternative intervention or a similar service in their locality. In such a situation, the real impact of the new intervention may be hidden.

External validity refers to the generalisability of results and is concerned with how representative the sample is of the real world situation. External validity can be enhanced by a pragmatic trial design, which involves the allocation of participants who are typical of usual service users and which attempts to mirror the provision of services in the real world (Roland and Torgerson, 1998).

Randomised controlled trials

The randomised controlled trial (RCT), based on a random allocation of subjects between the interventions under investigation, is widely accepted as the 'gold-standard' for clinical and economic evaluations (Woolfe *et al.*, 1990). Randomisation is a method of selection that ensures that every participant has an equal chance of being selected for entry into one arm of the trial or another. The aim of randomisation is to obtain two groups of participants that are similar in all respects other than the intervention and this is done by removing the possibility of any bias in allocation (Drummond *et al.*, 1999; Moser and Kalton, 1993). RCTs, therefore, tend to score high on validity, particularly if pragmatic, hence the preference for RCTs in clinical trials.

Other trial designs tend to be more limited in validity (Sackett *et al.*, 1985). Before-and-after studies, for example, are often used when the decision is made to replace one intervention with another before an assessment of effectiveness or cost-effectiveness can be carried out. Controlling for confounding factors in such studies is difficult since the comparison of groups within different time periods inevitably increases the likelihood of other political, social or environmental changes that may jeopardise internal validity. Similarly, comparisons between different localities, one with the new intervention and one without, will struggle to control for differences in socio-economic and demographic factors. Case-control studies can go some way to removing the problem of different time periods, particularly if attempts are made to match the groups on relevant indicators, such as age, sex and ethnic group, although it may still prove difficult to match participants on all relevant characteristics.

Obstacles to randomisation

There are a number of situations that preclude or hinder the use of a randomised, controlled design. Some are common to both health and social care, whilst others are more relevant to social care alone. In all fields, an RCT is impossible if the intervention is made universally available before an evaluation can take place, for example the provision of winter fuel payments to all state pension recipients. Similarly, where there is some urgency to the introduction of an intervention, such as new safety measures for the protection of children at risk of abuse, RCTs, which can take a number of years to complete, would be inappropriate. In addition, RCTs can be extremely expensive and lack of funds will often be a motivation for selecting an alternative trial design.

One widely cited criticism relates to the ethics of randomisation. It may, for example, be considered unethical to randomise when one intervention is believed to be less effective than the alternative. It is the provision of untested interventions, however, that should be considered unethical, since there is no evidence to suggest that the intervention is safe, effective or cost-effective (Williams, 1992). In general, an RCT which compares a new intervention to current best practice should be considered ethical where the professionals involved are ignorant of the relative value of the alternatives, and where all participants have given consent to randomisation based on appropriate information regarding the nature and purpose of the study and the potential risks and benefits involved (Pocock, 1983).

A further limitation is the impact of user preferences (Brewin and Bradley, 1989). Where users are unwilling to receive one of the interventions, they may refuse entry into a trial, thereby reducing the generalisability of the results and the potential sample size. In addition, the motivation of users who agree to randomisation even though they have a strong preference for one alternative may confound the trial results. In particular, those who do not receive their preferred choice may be demoralised to the extent that their outcomes are worse than those that would have occurred had they not had a particular preference. One solution is the use of 'patient-preference' trials, which involve the randomisation only of those people who do not have a strong preference before entry into the study (Torgerson *et al.*, 1996).

The heterogeneous nature of social care can add further obstacles to randomisation. Where complex packages of care are provided within a multi-disciplinary framework, controlling the interventions under investigation becomes difficult and internal validity is reduced, whilst local variations reduce the external validity of results. Whether or not such heterogeneity precludes the possibility of randomisation, however, must be assessed on a trial-by-trial basis. Randomised trials have been successfully carried out in extremely heterogeneous areas of mental health care, such as models of community care for people suffering from serious mental illness (UK700 Group, 1999; 2000), so this design should not be dismissed.

Qualitative research

In an attempt to explore the quantitative methods of analysis used in economic evaluation, little mention has been made of methods commonly employed in social care research, such as qualitative analysis. Far from reducing the importance of qualitative research, quantitative research should be seen as an additional tool for use in social care and the likelihood is that the most enlightening research would be produced by evaluations that encompass elements of both.

Although the RCT may produce the best evidence of the cost-effectiveness of competing interventions, quantitative research is limited in its ability to answer questions of how and why. This can be particularly limiting in the evaluation of complex packages of care, since it would be desirable to know which individual elements of care are beneficial and which categories of user benefit the most. Knowledge of quantitative analysis can enhance the scientific integrity and validity of the effectiveness and cost-effectiveness results produced, whilst qualitative analysis can look behind these results and disentangle questions of how, why and for whom an intervention works and under what circumstances.

Conclusion

As long as there is a mismatch between the demand for social care and the resources available to provide such care, the need for evaluation of both effectiveness and cost-effectiveness will remain. Given the philosophy of welfare economics – the desire to improve on total societal well-being by maximising the benefits yielded from limited resources – the inclusion of economics should not be seen as a threat or a replacement for traditional social care research methods, but as an additional tool to aid resource allocation decisions in a complex organisation. Nor should economic evaluation diminish the values of social care research, such as the central importance of the user perspective. The societal perspective takes into consideration both the costs borne by users and carers and the benefits gained. Service-use questionnaires can be developed with user and carer consultation whilst outcome measures can be designed with user and carer input into the description of relevant life states and their valuation. In addition, the use of patient-preference designs in randomised trials can add to the scientific integrity of studies, whilst allowing for the preferences of users to be incorporated. By adding to the strengths of social care research, economic analysis can provide valuable information to increase the benefits to users and carers, and to enhance the overall efficiency with which resources are allocated in the social care field.

Bibliography

Bannock, G., Baxter, R.E. and Rees, R. (1984) *The Penguin Dictionary of Economics*. Harmondsworth: Penguin Books Ltd

Beecham, J. (1995) 'Collecting and estimating costs', in M. Knapp (ed.) *The Economic Evaluation of Mental Health Care*. Canterbury: University of Kent

Beecham, J. and Knapp, M. (1992) 'Costing psychiatric interventions', in G. Thornicroft, C. Brewin and J. Wing (eds) *Measuring Mental Health Needs*. London: Royal College of Psychiatrists

Brewin, C.R. and Bradley, C. (1989) 'Patient preferences and randomised clinical trials', *British Medical Journal*, Vol. 299, pp. 313–15

Byford, S. and Raftery, J. (1998) 'Perspectives in economic evaluation', *British Medical Journal*, Vol. 316, p. 1529

Chartered Institute of Public Finance and Accountancy (CIPFA) (1998) *The Health Service Financial Database 1998*. London: CIPFA

Chartered Institute of Public Finance and Accountancy (CIPFA) (1999) *Personal Social Services Statistics 1997–98: Actuals*. London: CIPFA

Drummond, M.F. (1991) 'Output measurement for resource allocation decisions in health care', in A. McGuire, P. Fenn and K. Mayhew (eds) *Providing Health Care: the Economics of Alternative Systems of Finance and Delivery*. Oxford: Oxford University Press

Drummond, M.F., O'Brien, B., Stoddart, G.L. and Torrance, G.W. (1999) *Methods for the Economic Evaluation of Health Care Programmes*. Oxford: Oxford Medical Publications

Kavanagh, S. and Stewart, A. (1995) 'Economic evaluations of mental health care: modes and methods', in M. Knapp (ed.) *The Economic Evaluation of Mental Health Care*. Canterbury: University of Kent

Kind, P (1988) *The Design and Construction of Quality of Life Measures*. Discussion Paper No. 43. York: Centre for Health Economics

Koopmanschap, M.A. and Rutten, F.F.H. (1996) 'A practical guide for calculating indirect costs of disease', *Pharmacoeconomics*, Vol. 10, No. 5, pp. 460–6

Loomes, G and McKenzie, L. (1989) 'The use of QALYs in health care decision making', *Social Science and Medicine*, Vol. 28, pp. 299–308

Luce, B.R. and Elixhauser, A. (1990) 'Estimating costs in the economic evaluation of medical technologies', *International Journal of Technology Assessment in Health Care*, Vol. 6, pp. 57–75

McGuire, A., Henderson, J. and Mooney, G. (1992) *The Economics of Health Care: an Introductory Text*. London: Routledge

Mauskopf, J., Schulman, K., Bell, L. and Glick, H. (1996) 'A strategy for collecting pharmacoeconomic data during phase II/III clinical trials', *Pharmacoeconomics*, Vol. 9, No. 3, pp. 264–77

Moser, C.A. and Kalton, G. (1993) *Survey Methods in Social Investigation*. Aldershot: Dartmouth Publishing Company

Netten, A. and Beecham, J. (1993) *Costing Community Care*. Canterbury: University of Kent

Netten, A., Dennett, J. and Knight, J. (1999) *Unit Costs of Health and Social Care*. Canterbury: University of Kent

Pocock, S.J. (1983) *Clinical Trials: a Practical Approach*. Chichester: John Wiley & Sons

Robinson, R. (1993a) 'Economic evaluation and health care: the policy context', *British Medical Journal*, Vol. 307, pp. 994–6

Robinson, R. (1993b) 'Economic evaluation and health care: costs and cost-minimisation analysis', *British Medical Journal*, Vol. 307, pp. 726–8

Robinson, R. (1993c) 'Economic evaluation and health care: cost-effectiveness analysis', *British Medical Journal*, Vol. 307, pp. 793–5

Robinson, R. (1993d) 'Economic evaluation and health care: cost-utility analysis', *British Medical Journal*, Vol. 307, pp. 859–62

Robinson, R. (1993e) 'Economic evaluation and health care: cost-benefit analysis', *British Medical Journal*, Vol. 307, pp. 924–6

Roland, M. and Torgerson, D.J. (1998) 'Understanding controlled trials: what are pragmatic trials?', *British Medical Journal*, Vol. 316, p. 285

Sackett, D.L., Haynes, R.B. and Tugwell, P. (1985) 'Clinical epidemiology: a basic science for clinical medicine', Boston: Little, Brown & Co.

Torgerson, D.J., Klaber-Moffett, J. and Russell, I.T. (1996) 'Including patient preferences in randomised clinical trials', *Journal of Health Services Research and Policy*, Vol. 20, pp. 637–48

UK700 Group (Burns, T., Creed, F., Fahy, T., Thompson, S., Tyrer, P. and White, I.) (1999) 'Intensive versus standard case management for severe psychotic illness: a randomised trial', *The Lancet*, Vol. 353, pp. 2185–9

UK700 Group (Byford, S., Fiander, M., Torgerson, D.J., Barber, J.A., Thompson, S.G., Burns, T., van Horn, E., Gilvarry, C. and Creed, F.) (2000) 'Cost-effectiveness of intensive versus standard case management for severe psychotic illness: UK700 case management trial', *British Journal of Psychiatry*, Vol. 176, pp. 537–43

Williams, A. (1992) 'Cost-effectiveness analysis: is it ethical?', *Journal of Medical Ethics*, Vol. 18, No. 1, pp. 7–11

Williams, A. and Kind, P. (1992) 'The present state of play about QALYs', in A. Hopkins (ed.) *Measures of Quality of Life*. London: Royal College of Physicians

Woolfe, S.H., Battista, R.N. and Anderson, G.M. *et al.* (1990) 'Assessing the clinical effectiveness of preventive manoeuvres: analytic principles and systematic methods in reviewing evidence and developing clinical practice recommendations', *Journal of Clinical Epidemiology*, Vol. 43, pp. 891–905

6 Applying Economic Approaches and Concepts to Independent Living

Ann Netten

Introduction

Issues of scarcity are increasingly relevant to supporting independent living. This is because there are high and rising costs of health and social care, together with the possibility of declining abilities of society to meet these costs. Knapp (1999) identifies six trends with implications for increasing pressure on resources:

- *Demographic changes*, such as rises in the proportion of people over 80 years of age, changes in female labour force participation rates and geographical mobility, which affect the availability of informal care-giving support.

- *Expenditure cuts by government or other funders*: for example, local authorities must deal with competing demands for resources while central government has set targets for 2 and 3 per cent improvements in 'efficiency' of English local authorities over three financial years.

- *Policy and practice changes* that move responsibilities between government departments or between public and private sectors: for example, the reduced role of hospitals in providing continuing care places added to pressures on care homes and community services.

- *Raised expectations held by the general public*: most people expect the standards of service from public and other agencies to improve over time, even though, as taxpayers, they may want to limit the levels of their tax contributions.

- *Higher standards* of service also tend to be expected by professionals such as geriatricians, social workers and others. These groups quite rightly want to improve the accessibility and quality of the services they offer to their clients.

- *Increasingly high expectations from service users, and their relatives or carers*: during the last ten to 15 years there has been a rapid development of advocacy movements representing users and carers. The effect is almost always to put further pressure on resources.

So, pressures are resulting both from reduced resources and increased demands on those resources.

Efficient and cost-effective use of available resources is a sensible objective. It is only ethical that we should aim to use the resources available to gain the most benefit for the most people. By definition, economic concepts and approaches have much to offer us in addressing this objective. This paper starts by considering some of the ways in which lessons from economics have been translated into public policy in recent years. Economic frameworks that have been used in evaluative research are described and the implications of these for evaluating the cost-effectiveness of independent living are discussed.

Use of economics in policies about independent living

Since the post-war development of public services, such as the NHS, the issue of restraining public expenditure has been a major one when considering how best to meet the needs of people with impairments. Concepts from economics were overtly introduced to policies concerned with people with impairments in the early 1980s in the UK Government's Financial Management Initiative (FMI) and by the Audit Commission. Economy, effectiveness and efficiency, or the 'three Es', underpinned the value-for-money drives of that time, and ran through performance reviews and similar initiatives of subsequent years.

Knapp (1995) points out that the fourth 'E' – equity (or distributive justice) – is sometimes overlooked but is clearly relevant to public social services. One interpretation of equity is successful targeting of resources on needs, which has allocative efficiency implications. Horizontal efficiency occurs when services are allocated to all those with relevant needs. Vertical efficiency occurs when those who have most potential to benefit are allocated more services than those with lower-level requirements.

A fundamental economic premise is that, given choice and information, individuals will maximise their utility (or benefit) within the restraints of the resources available to them. By definition, therefore, individuals are efficient in obtaining outcomes from resources. Thus, introducing choice and information about resources available and the costs of different options should lead to the more efficient use of resources. The Independent Living Fund (ILF) and direct payments, which allow individuals themselves to decide how their care budget is spent, could be represented as most closely empowering the consumer to maximise the benefit from resources. But the policies introduced in the 1989 White Paper (Cm. 849, 1989) and subsequent legislation also demonstrate these principles in a number of ways:

- *The purchaser–provider split*: introducing the concept of purchasers who can identify alternative providers, and thus provide choice, mirroring the consumer market place.

- *Care management with devolved budgets*: improving information both about resources available and costs of different options, together with flexibility in using resources to meet needs.

- *Promoting the mixed economy of care*: encouraging a variety of providers to enhance choice and competition, which would be expected to keep prices down.

- *Targeting of resources on those in greatest need*: there was a particular emphasis at this time on improving vertical target efficiency through concentrating resources on 'flexible and intensive personal care services for people who would otherwise require institutional care'(Cm. 849, 1989, para. 3.6.3).

Current policies in the field of social care have not turned their back on these, but emphasise independence, regulation and standards (Cm. 4169, 1998). Moreover, there is increased emphasis on the need for low-level 'preventative' packages of care. The vertical efficiency argument is represented more in terms of capacity to benefit through longer-term outcomes and subsequent reductions of needs for services.

However, the policies are being implemented in the context of the 'Best Value' initiative in local government, which emphasises the policy of maximising cost-effectiveness in the use of public money. Moreover, within the Performance Assessment Framework, a key tool in 'raising standards', there are nine cost-based performance indicators. The commentary surrounding these makes it clear that lower levels of cost are seen as a desirable objective in improving efficiency. While there are indicators of 'Effectiveness of service delivery and outcomes' these are primarily process indicators, such as use of intensive home care and numbers of people receiving services. Behind the Best Value targeted indicator of costs of intensive care for adults,[1] there lies the assumption that keeping people in their own homes is both less costly and a better outcome for people.

While it easy to criticise the application of the approach, in practice the overall objective of improving the benefits derived from resources is a desirable one. But, with such powerful incentives at work to reduce costs, and with relatively clumsy indicators of outcome, it is essential that we analyse in more depth the relationship between costs, standards, quality and outcomes. Evaluative research can provide valuable information in this process. In undertaking such research, it is helpful to have frameworks to help establish what we should be measuring and how.

Economic frameworks for independent living

The Production of Welfare approach has been developed as a conceptual framework for social care services for adults (Davies and Knapp, 1981; Knapp, 1984, 1995). Figure 6.1 shows how this framework distinguishes five key elements in the process of producing care:

- *resource inputs*: principally staff time, aids and adaptations, and buildings required for services such as day centres

- the *costs* of these inputs measured in financial terms

- *non-resource inputs,* which are factors that affect outcomes but do not have a measurable cost, such as staff attitudes and social care environments

- *intermediate outcomes*, which are produced by services and include measures of the volumes of services (such as number of home care hours) and less easily measured factors (such as quality of care)

- *final outcomes*, which are changes over time in the well-being (welfare) and quality of life of users of services.

This approach helps us to define efficiency, effectiveness and equity in terms of the component elements of the framework. It assists in considering and analysing the complex combination of factors that are likely to influence the effectiveness of any one service or intervention.

The framework has been used in the evaluation of community care services for elderly people (Challis *et al.*, 1995; Davies *et al.*, 1990, 2000) and mental health services (Knapp *et al.*, 1992, 1998). The approach underpinned the evaluation of the pilot case management schemes (Challis *et al.*, 1995; Davies and Challis, 1986) to examine how different support arrangements and resources produced user and care-giver outcomes. It could be

Figure 6.1 The Production of Welfare

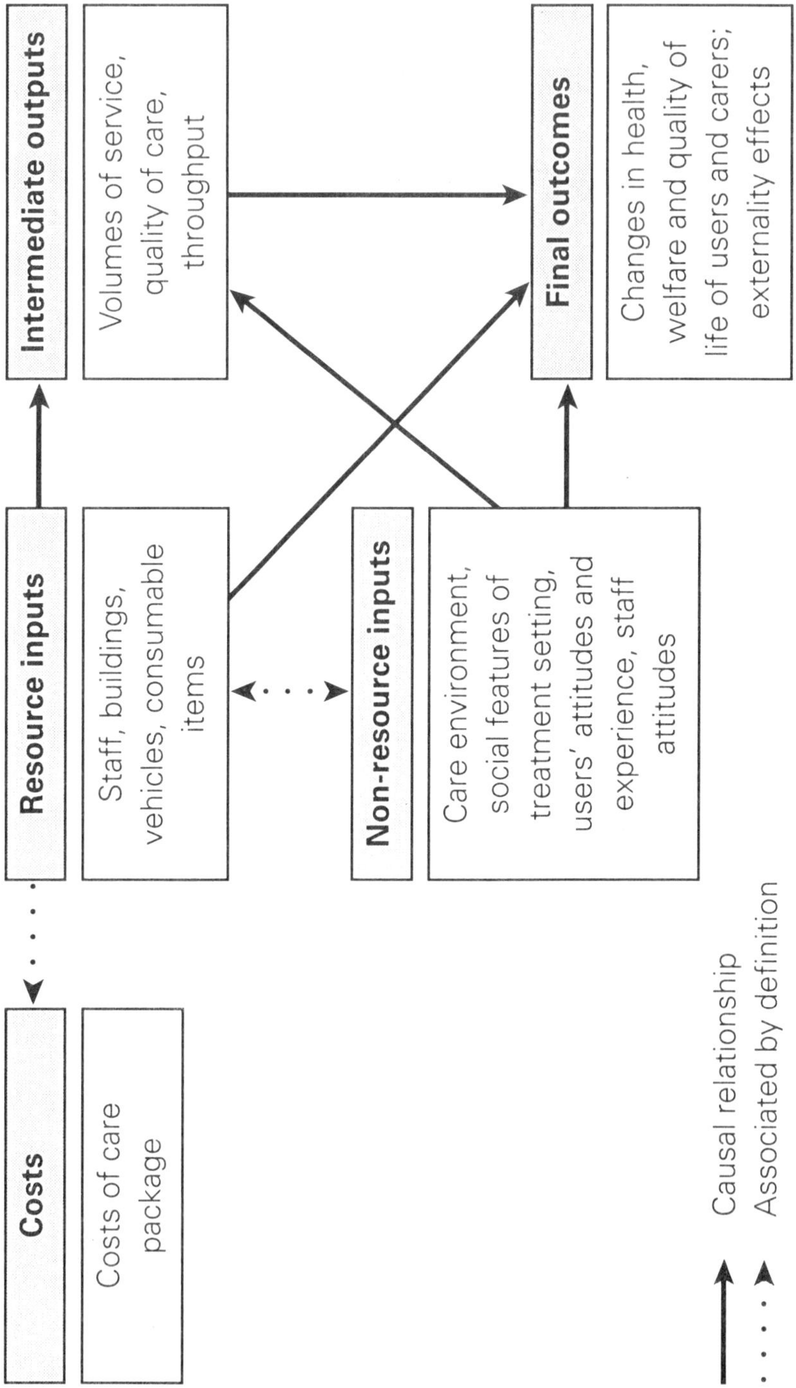

Costs	Costs of care package
Resource inputs	Staff, buildings, vehicles, consumable items
Non-resource inputs	Care environment, social features of treatment setting, users' attitudes and experience, staff attitudes
Intermediate outputs	Volumes of service, quality of care, throughput
Final outcomes	Changes in health, welfare and quality of life of users and carers; externality effects

Causal relationship
Associated by definition

argued that these studies were so influential because of their ability to demonstrate improved efficiency: better outcomes could be achieved by maintaining people in their own homes at the same level of resources that would otherwise be used for residential care.

A development of the framework that puts the individuals with impairments at the heart of our thinking rather than taking the service-oriented approach is called the Social Production of Welfare (Netten and Davies, 1990) illustrated in Figure 6.2.

This framework draws on a branch of economics termed household economics (Becker, 1965; Lancaster, 1966), which represents households as units of production. The overall objective is to produce well-being or utility for members of the household through what are termed 'commodities', such as nutrition, social interaction and so on. In the process, the household uses resources at its disposal: primarily the time of household members, physical facilities and unearned income. These resources are used to generate income, to purchase goods and services, and to produce 'commodities' directly.

The effect of impairment on the household is to change what individuals do and contribute to the household, and to increase the demand for commodities such as personal comfort. Thus, for example, if an individual breaks their leg, they may no longer be able to prepare meals and may need help getting dressed. Long-term severe impairment can mean the resources of the household can no longer produce enough for household members, so people from other households get routinely involved in helping out. Thus, the unit of production for social care becomes the informal care network.

In this framework, the individual with impairment and other members of the care network are both producers and consumers of commodities. The key elements are as before:

Figure 6.2 The Social Production of Welfare

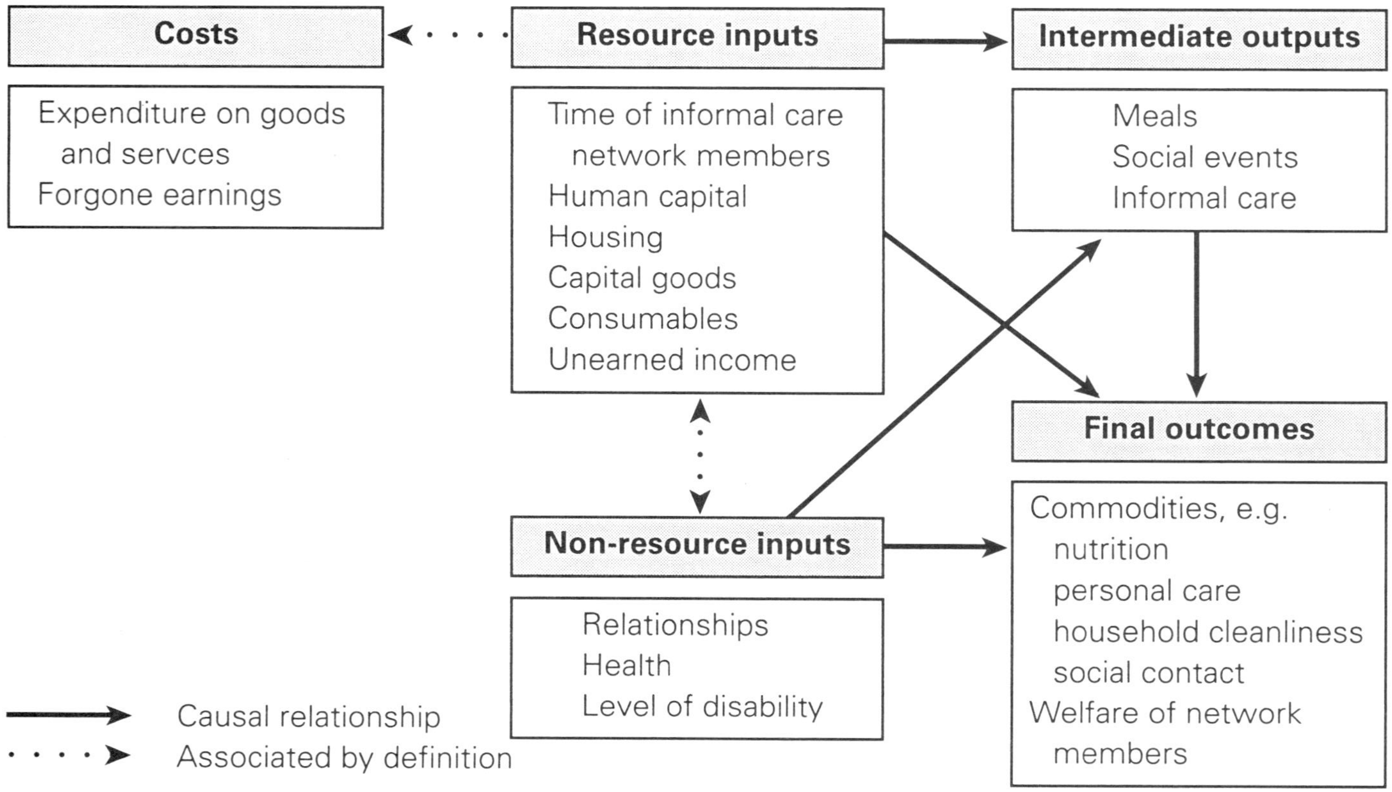

Costs	Expenditure on goods and serveces Forgone earnings
Resource inputs	Time of informal care network members Human capital Housing Capital goods Consumables Unearned income
Intermediate outputs	Meals Social events Informal care
Non-resource inputs	Relationships Health Level of disability
Final outcomes	Commodities, e.g. nutrition personal care household cleanliness social contact Welfare of network members

Causal relationship

Associated by definition

- *resource inputs*: the time of informal care network members, physical facilities, unearned income, and goods and services

- *costs*: the opportunity costs of informal care in addition to expenditure on goods and services

- *non-resource inputs*: including attitudes and relationships between members of the household

- *intermediate outcomes*: including meals produced and social events

- *final outcomes*: as before incorporating well-being of individuals but also including benefit derived from commodities.

This approach means we can define the role of government-funded inputs in terms of their expected effects:

- *Financial contributions such as direct payments*: add directly to the resources of the network and enable household members to purchase goods and services.

- *Aids and adaptations*: improve the productivity of individuals with impairment.

- *Home care workers*: substitute for household members by undertaking personal care tasks.

- *Meals services*: supply intermediate outcomes directly to the household.

- *Social work interventions*: can contribute to the technical efficiency of the care network in enabling individuals to access services and through advocacy and counselling.

- *Respite and day care services*: reduce the demand for help within the network.

- *Care management*: increases the efficiency of service inputs by appropriate assessment, monitoring and matching of needs to resources.

- *Training carers*: contributes to the 'human capital' or skills available to the household.

- *Residential care*: virtually replaces the entire production process.

The framework has been used in developing approaches to estimating the costs of informal care and measuring outcomes (described below).

Costs

The experience of applying the Production of Welfare framework in a variety of evaluations led Knapp (1993) to identify four key 'rules' when undertaking costs research. These can be summarised as:

- comprehensive and accurate measurement

- identifying and exploring variation

- comparing like with like

- integrating cost information with outcomes.

Comprehensive and accurate measurement

Basic economic principles of opportunity costing described by Sarah Byford in Chapter 5 of this volume mean that the way costs are measured depends on the purpose of the costing exercise and the perspective that is being taken. Within these limits, it is critical to measure the resource implications comprehensively if appropriate conclusions are to be drawn.

Often the primary focus will be the cost to the public purse. Government expenditure supporting independent living is associated with a number of different agencies:

- Department of Health (DH) policy and local authority purchase and provision of social care

- local authority housing departments' provision of sheltered and specialised housing

- independent sector provision of social care and housing services

- Department of Social Security (DSS) welfare payments

- NHS community and primary care services

- Department of Transport, the Environment and the Regions (DETR) and local authority responsibility for transport services

- Department for Education and Employment (DfEE) provision of training and education.

Each of these agencies has different, if overlapping, objectives in supporting independent living. Social care is concerned with the impact of impairment on people's lives, with social care services compensating for handicap. Health services are primarily concerned with treating the causes of impairment. Housing services are primarily concerned with shelter and providing a facilitative environment. Public transport services should (at least in theory) be concerned with facilitating people with impairment in getting around. Education and employment services are concerned with enhancing individuals' abilities to participate in the workforce.

So, for example, for an older person with severe arthritis, the NHS might provide a replacement hip and medication. Social care services would be concerned with the impact of reduced mobility on the individual's ability to get their meals, whether they were becoming socially isolated, whether they were safe and whether they could care for themselves. These issues would be affected by the type of housing they were living in and the degree to which transport services enabled them to get to the shops and so on. Of course, the degree to which all these factors affected the individual would be dependent on the nature and extent of their informal care support network.

If all these factors are related to the success with which an individual can be supported in independent living, then it is important to identify the costs of these inputs, or at least to allow for them in analyses. This then raises the issue of who bears the cost. Health care costs (with the exception of nursing home care) are borne by the State. Social care costs are borne by local authorities and private individuals in the fees that they pay. Depending on the perspective taken, housing and transportation costs are borne by private individuals, the DSS, local authorities and social care services. Although it could be argued that benefits such as Attendance Allowance compensate for informal care costs, the vast majority of these costs are borne by the carers themselves.

Once we have identified what costs we should measure, the next step is to consider how we should measure them. For estimation purposes there are two principal types of cost relevant to independent living: services and informal care.

Measuring the costs of services

In order to estimate direct costs of service provison there are four key stages (Allen and Beecham, 1993):

- describe the service
- identify the activities being undertaken
- identify the resource implications
- calculate total and unit costs.

Describing the service and fully understanding what is produced and how is a fundamental first step in any costing exercise. Once this is established, accurate measurement of service inputs depends on matching resource use information appropriately to activities. There are two principal ways of estimating costs:

- a *top-down approach*, which divides expenditure by activity
- a *bottom-up approach*, which builds up all the elements of cost associated with a given activity.

The top-down approach is used in all the performance indicators described above and is useful when monitoring costs over time. The Chartered Institute of Public Finance and

Accountancy (CIPFA) produces regular unit costs for local authority purchased and provided services estimated on this basis (see for example, CIPFA, 1999). The Department of Health (DH) estimates key indicator unit costs on the basis of expenditure information provided by local authorities in Revenue Out-turn returns to DETR and routine activity data collections of the DH (Department of Health, 1999). In both cases, services tend to be grouped together and reflect overall averages of a wide range of types of provision. The performance indicators are largely based on the Department of Health key indicators. This top-down approach is also used to estimate the costs of hospital care using returns to the NHS Executive (Netten *et al.*, 1999).

The principal problem with the top-down approach is that, when using the information, it is a bit like a 'black box'. It is not clear whether all the relevant costs have been identified and whether all the activities that are responsible for the expenditure have been measured. Thus, for example, the costs of local authority residential care could include or exclude the overhead management costs of the authority and the costs of day care and other services provided for non-residents. In a research evaluation that estimates the costs of a service from scratch this is less of a problem, but it is important to ensure that resources are disaggregated to appropriate measures of output (see Bebbington, 1993 for an example).

The bottom-up approach to estimating unit costs identifies all the resources associated with, and necessary for, specific service activities. This is more transparent, so those using the information can adapt it to suit local circumstances and the perspective of a costing exercise. This approach is used wherever possible in *Unit Costs of Health and Social Care* (Netten *et al.*, 1999), which has been produced annually since 1994. However, the approach has its own problems. It is difficult to establish good information about overhead costs, and these costs are often very approximate. Beecham (2000) has recently produced a very helpful guide to the process, which, although it is described in the context of services for children in need, is equally applicable to adult services.

Costs should be estimated for a specific evaluation reflecting the actual resources used and the prices of those resources. Prices of independent sector services charged to local authorities can be used as reasonable proxies for costs in most circumstances as they reflect the cost to the purchaser. However, in some circumstances, prices may not reflect costs. For example, voluntary agencies may subsidise prices charged to individuals when the service is not purchased through a local authority and large organisations may cross-subsidise between services. The cost should be estimated whenever there is likely to be a substantial difference between the price and the cost.

However, the resource implications of collecting detailed cost information are sometimes not justified. This occurs when, for example, the service concerned is of relatively minor importance in the evaluation, or the problems associated with estimating local costs become excessive. In such situations, the detailed information in the *Unit Costs of Health and Social Care* series means that the estimates can be used and adapted to reflect the perspective of a specific study.

Costing informal care

It is widely acknowledged that the majority of the costs of maintaining people in their own homes fall to the informal sector. But the costs of this input are mostly indirect and rarely measured. Moreover, when they are considered, it is often a very partial picture that is presented. The Social Production of Welfare framework described above provides a useful starting point for considering the potential costs that could arise both to carers and to society as a whole.

Netten (1993) describes a comprehensive approach to costing informal care. The opportunity costs that can be incurred by informal carers include:

- time spent on caring tasks

- accommodation changes made as a result of impairment (for example, older people moving in with their children)

- financial expenditure including, for example, travel and additional heating bills

- future expectations when carers' careers or working lives have been affected (for example, by giving up waged work or reducing hours on a permanent basis).

Informal care costs present problems both in identifying the level of resources used as a result of caring responsibilities and in attaching values to these resources. The only direct cost identified above is financial where the problem is restricted to identifying expenditure associated with caring responsibilities. However, direct expenditure tends to be a relatively small proportion of the total opportunity cost borne by carers. The largest single component is usually the time of individuals.

The measurement of how much time is due to caring responsibilities as opposed to the ongoing relationship is not always easy for individuals to identify and presents problems of reliability when measured as part of an evaluation. The valuation of this time depends on what would have been done with the time in the absence of impairment and whether the perspective is that of society or of the individual carer.

The principal divide in terms of type of time is between waged and unwaged time. Waged time can be valued in terms of lost income to individual carers or lost productivity to society. There is not sufficient space here to discuss all the issues involved in the valuation of unwaged time, which have been debated elsewhere (see, for example, Brouwer, 1999; Posnett and Jan, 1996). However, given the high proportion of time that is spent on caring outside the normal working week and the high proportion of carers who are retired, it is important that this input is valued appropriately. Netten (1993) presents an argument for using a 'shadow price' of the domestic wage rate for unwaged time.

The principles of opportunity costing allow us to value the accommodation 'lost' to a carer as the rent that the carer could have obtained if they let out the accommodation. From society's perspective, however, there may be no loss (or even a gain) as the accommodation given up by the older person would be released to be used by somebody else.

The long-term implications of giving up paid work, changing number of hours worked or losing opportunities for promotion again depend on the perspective taken. From the carer's point of view, there is the lost expected future stream of income; from society's perspective, there is the loss of what would have been produced. There is currently some debate about the most appropriate approach to take to measuring lost productivity (see Brouwer, 1999). The human capital approach calculates the future stream of productivity measured by the expected gross wage (the cost of employment to the employer) over the expected working life. The friction cost approach just measures the lost productivity during the period required to recruit and train an individual up to the same level of productivity as the individual who left the workforce.

Once we have identified comprehensive and accurate costs, the next step is interpretation.

Identifying and exploring variation in costs

There are two main reasons why estimated costs will vary. The first is uncertainty. Basic economic principles mean that there is no one 'gold-standard' cost of a service or package of care. Assumptions made in the course of estimation may be open to question and need to be tested to check what the implications are of different assumptions. Moreover, the types of distribution often found in cost data (very skewed with many people with relatively low cost packages and a few very high cost cases) mean that large samples (often very difficult to establish in social care research) are needed to predict costs with any confidence.

This makes it all the more important that substantive causes of variation in costs are investigated. In Chapter 5 of this volume, Sarah Byford describes the techniques that can be utilised in economics to explore cost variation, some of which have been used in production of welfare studies (see, for example, Knapp et al., 1998). Transferring these techniques to independent living raises the question: what are the causes of variation suggested by the theoretical frameworks and their empirical applications?

The causes of variation that should be investigated can be summarised as five key questions:

- *Who is being cared for?* The needs and characteristics of individuals are important determinants of the level of resources required, so variations in these would be expected to be associated with cost differences.

- *What is being produced?* In Production of Welfare terms, variations in intermediate outcomes, such as quality of care, would be expected to be associated with variations in costs. As discussed later, we would also expect the level of final outcomes or well-being to be associated with the costs of care.

- *In what circumstances?* Non-resource inputs, such as relationships between people with impairment and other members of the care network, staff attitudes and life events may impact on costs of supporting independent living. Where the costs of potential substitutes (such as informal care) and complements (such as health care) have not been included in the cost estimates, indicators of these inputs should be included as these will impact on the costs of social care. Environmental factors such as housing and public transport services will also affect the need for and costs of care.

- *Under what conditions?* Every producer and purchaser faces certain market conditions over which they have little control. These include factor prices (for example, local wage rates), the relationship between different factor prices and level of competition. Other non-market environmental factors, such as rurality of an area, will affect the costs of production.

- *How is care produced?* Scale of organisations and management of care will have cost implications. For example, local authority managed home care services traditionally provide better terms and conditions for staff and have to bear higher levels of overhead costs than independent services. Care management will have an impact on the organisation and co-ordination of care and costs of care packages.

Comparing like with like

It is a basic tenet of all good research practice that like should be compared with like in any evaluation of 'What works best?' A properly designed randomised controlled trial ensures that causes of variation associated with individual characteristics and circumstances should be adequately controlled for in any comparison. However, although this approach is often used in health services research, it is less acceptable and, it could be argued, applicable in many social welfare situations. In her discussion of methods of economic evaluations in social welfare, Holtermann (1998) reviews the evidence about the rigour with which research has been conducted into effectiveness of interventions. She concludes that there are relatively few studies, especially in the UK, that ensure that the question 'What works best?' can be reliably answered. By implication, potential causes of cost variation will not have been adjusted for, so direct cost comparisons made in such studies would not be valid.

Over and above this, there are particular implications when estimating and analysing cost information. The costs of some services, such as residential care, include the costs of accommodation and living expenses. If legitimate comparison is to be made with care delivered to people in their own home, it is important that these costs of living are also included in the estimation of costs of living independently.

In making like-with-like comparisons, the ultimate objective is to implement the final cost 'rule' identified above: integrating cost information with outcomes.

Outcomes

The ultimate aim in an economic evaluation is to identify the costs of achieving particular outcomes. Social care is fundamentally about meeting the needs of individuals in a way that maximises their independence. Independence is a term that is defined and interpreted in a wide variety of ways depending on perspective. For many healthy active older people, it is defined as being able to look after yourself on a daily basis without the need to resort to any support or assistance from others (Hayden *et al.*, 1999). It is obviously of prime importance that people should be enabled to do as much as possible unaided, but there are also benefits that need to be measured which are about compensating for impairment. Thus, while it is desirable that people should be able to prepare their own meals, it is also important that, by whatever means, they should receive an adequate, varied diet with meals at times that suit them. Moreover, disabled people frequently define independence in terms of control over how and when things are done rather than doing things themselves (Oliver, 1993).

In the Social Production of Welfare, from a publicly funded care perspective, the key issues that need to be addressed in evaluating the outcomes of independent living are whether the 'commodities' of concern are being produced to an adequate level. Key (or basic) commodities or aspects of life will be those that enable the individual and the informal care network to continue to function. In other words, these are the aspects of life that are likely to have long-term implications for individuals' mental or physical health.

There are two ways of identifying basic commodities: consult with people with impairments or consult with those concerned with the provision of care. Qureshi (1999) consulted users of services and identified very similar areas of concern as a consultation exercise undertaken as part of an ongoing Department of Health funded project (Netten and Smith, 1998). This took a top-down perspective and identified five domains of concern. In each case, it is possible to identify the high-level needs that would have long-term health implications:

- *Meals and nutrition*: long-term dietary problems have serious health implications especially for older people.

- *Personal comfort*: physical problems such as bedsores and burns can result from inadequate personal care, especially where there is incontinence.

- *Social participation and involvement*: isolation has been shown to be associated with dementia, mortality and morbidity.

- *Safety*: both in terms of objective measures of probability of physical or mental harm resulting from specific events, and in terms of long-term mental health effects of feeling insecure and afraid.

- *Control over daily living*: this has been identified above as a key aspect of independence. Moreover, a lack of sense of control over daily living can result in mental health problems in the long term and is intimately bound up in people's sense of what independence means, regardless of levels of ability.

This is not to imply that social care agencies are concerned only with very high levels of need with these long-term implications, or have no concerns beyond these core domains. But it is these areas of people's lives where social care is focused, because they are fundamental to individuals' well-being. Thus, it is these areas where we need to identify the benefit of welfare derived from social care interventions.

Once we are clear about the general objectives of care we then need to incorporate the client perspective on these objectives. There are two aspects to this:

- what the individual sees as the key issues within the domains

- the relative importance of the domains and levels of met need within the domains.

Thus, for example, some older people would find living in a house which was not clean and tidy undermined their sense of control (Clark *et al.*, 1988), whereas others may not be concerned about this, but would feel very strongly about having choice over when and what care was provided. The Quality of Life Assessment Schedule (QOLAS) (Selai *et al.*, 2000) identifies core domains and then allows individuals to identify what is most important to them within those domains and rate themselves against these individually defined aspects of health or well-being. This makes a very sensitive measure that reflects individual perspectives. However, as the measure currently stands, it still weights each domain equally.

In order to reflect the benefit gained from an intervention, we need to weight a measure to reflect the relative impact (or utility gained) of having needs met in one domain rather than another.

Thus, for example, control over daily life may be rated as more important than feeling safe and secure. If this were the case, the outcomes of individuals who stay in their own home in spite of a sense of risk would be measured as greater than those who move into residential care and feel more safe but less in control of their life. In the absence of any such weighting, the outcomes would be measured as having the same level of benefit.

Current work is examining the relative importance that older people attach to the domains of social care (Netten and Smith, 1998). However, in evaluating independent living more broadly, these domains may appear too limited. The Schedule for the Evaluation of Individual Quality of Life (SEIQoL) (O'Boyle *et al.*, 1993) allows individuals to nominate the domains they consider most important to their quality of life and to use their own value system when describing the relative importance of those domains. The first approach used to establish preferences (judgement analysis) is complicated and impractical for people with cognitive impairment. Another approach (direct weighting) has been developed which is easier (Browne *et al.*, 1997). The results of the two approaches are not interchangeable and more work is needed. However, this approach might have potential uses for identifying well-being or utility outcomes of independent living.

A particular challenge of measuring outcomes in independent living is the fact that in many cases there are outcomes for more than one individual: in particular, principal carers. Ideally, a measure of outcome would incorporate the carer's utility as well as the benefit gained by the person with impairment. This is particularly relevant when services are primarily aimed at relieving carers, so any measured outcomes for the individual are minimal, or even negative.

Conclusion

Alan Milburn gave a speech at the LSE in which he demonstrated the importance of viewing spending on the NHS as an investment in the productivity of the workforce and national economic success (Milburn, 2000). The speech represented a welcome change in approach to health expenditure. The application of this argument to long-term impairments associated with older age groups and impairments that prevent people from participating in the workforce is more limited, although there are issues about the degree to which carers can participate in the workforce. Mostly, however, increased levels of efficiency in health and social care for older people and those with impairments are very much the order of the day.

Efficiency is an appropriate and ethical aim as it means that we use our resources in a way to generate the most benefit. Policy makers, in the drive to improve efficiency, have adopted economic concepts and approaches. However, using broad indicators of performance will not reflect the full picture and may conceal perverse incentives. Detailed economic evaluation is needed in order that we can understand the relationship between costs, standards, and quality and outcomes. It is important to be clear, however, that economic evaluation does not make the decisions; it just makes them better informed.

Economic frameworks have already been developed that can help us define the key variables that we need to consider and their expected relationships. These make it clear that it is important in economic evaluations of independent living to take into account non-resource issues, such as attitudes and relationships, and to measure the costs both of services and of informal care. There is considerable work to draw on in the estimation and use of cost information. However, there is much to be done in a key aspect of evaluation: the measurement of outcomes in a way that can be incorporated into economic studies.

Note

1   Acknowledged as problematic in that the measures of expenditure and activity are not matched (Department of Health, 1999).

Bibliography

Allen, C. and Beecham, J. (1993) 'Costing services: ideals and reality', in A. Netten and J. Beecham (eds) *Costing Community Care Theory and Practice*. Aldershot: Ashgate

Bebbington, A. (1993) 'Costing a centre for AIDS/HIV', in A. Netten and J. Beecham (eds) *Costing Community Care Theory and Practice*. Aldershot: Ashgate

Becker, G. (1965) 'A theory of the allocation of time', *The Economic Journal*, September

Beecham, J. (2000) *Unit Costs – not exactly Child's Play*. Canterbury: Department of Health, Dartington Social Services and the Personal Social Services Research Unit, University of Kent at Canterbury

Brouwer, W.B.F. (1999) *Time and Time Costs in Economic Evaluation: Taking a Societal Perspective*. Ridderkerk: W.B.F. Brouwer/Ridderprint

Browne, J.P., O'Boyle, C.A., McGee, H.M., McDonald, N.J. and Joyce, C.R.B. (1997) 'Development of a direct weighting procedure for quality of life domains', *Quality of Life Research*, Vol. 6, pp. 301–9

Challis, D., Darton, R., Johnson, L., Stone, M. and Traske, K. (1995) *Care Management and Health Care of Older People*. Aldershot: Arena

Clark, H., Dyer, S. and Horwood, J. (1988) *'That Bit of Help': The High Value of Low Level Preventative Services for Older People*. Bristol: The Policy Press/JRF

Chartered Institute of Public Finance and Accountancy (CIPFA) (1999) *Personal Social Services Statistics 1998: Actuals*. London: Statistical Information Service

Cm. 849 (1989) *Caring for People: Community Services in the Next Decade and Beyond*. London: HMSO

Cm. 4169 (1998) *Modernising Social Services: Promoting Independence, Improving Protection, Raising Standards.* London: The Stationery Office

Davies, B. and Challis, D. (1986) *Matching Resources to Needs in Community Care.* Aldershot: Ashgate

Davies, B. and Fernandez, J., with Nomer, B. (2000) *Equity and Efficiency in Policy in Community Care.* Aldershot: Ashgate

Davies, B.P. and Knapp, M.R.J. (1981) *Old People's Homes and the Production of Welfare.* London: Routledge

Davies, B., Bebbington, A. and Charnley, H. (1990) *Resources, Needs and Outcomes in Community-based Care.* Aldershot: Ashgate

Department of Health (1999) *Key Indicators Graphical System, Updates.* London: Department of Health

Fratiglioni, L., Wang, H.-X., Ericsson, K., Maytan, M. and Winblad, B. (2000) 'Influence of social network on occurrence of dementia: a community-based longitudinal study', *The Lancet,* Vol. 355, 15 April

Hayden, C., Boaz, A. and Taylor, F. (1999) *Attitudes and Aspirations of Older People: a Qualitative Study.* Research Report No. 102. London: Department of Social Security

Holtermann, S. (1998) *Weighing it up.* York: Joseph Rowntree Foundation

Knapp, M.R.J. (1984) *The Economics of Social Care.* London: Macmillan

Knapp, M. (1993) 'Principles of applied cost research', in A. Netten and J. Beecham (eds) *Costing Community Care Theory and Practice.* Aldershot: Ashgate

Knapp, M. (1995) 'The economic perspective: framework and principles' in M. Knapp (ed.) *The Economic Evaluation of Mental Health Care.* Aldershot: Arena

Knapp, M. (1999) 'Economics and the care of older people: Why? When? How? And with what future prospects?', PSSRU Discussion Paper No. 1530, Personal Social Services Research Unit, London School of Economics. Submitted for publication to the *Hong Kong Journal of Gerontology*

Knapp, M., Cambridge, P., Thomason, C., Beecham, J., Allen, C. and Darton, R. (1992) *Care in the Community: Challenge and Demonstration.* Aldershot: Ashgate

Knapp, M., Marks, I., Wolstenholme, J., Beecham, J., Astin, J., Audini, B., Connolly, J. and Watts, V. (1998) 'Home-based *versus* hospital-based care for serious mental illness', *British Journal of Psychiatry,* Vol. 172, pp. 506–12

Lancaster, K. (1966) 'A new approach to consumer theory', *Journal of Political Economy,* Vol. 74, pp.132–57

Lawton, M.P. (1975) 'The Philadelphia Geriatric Centre morale scale: a revision', *Journal of Gerontology*, Vol. 30, No. 1, pp. 85–9

Milburn, A. (2000) 'A healthier nation and a healthier economy: the contribution of a modern NHS', LSE Health Annual Lecture, 8 March

Netten, A. (1993) 'Costing informal care', in A. Netten and J. Beecham (eds) *Costing Community Care Theory and Practice*. Aldershot: Ashgate

Netten, A. and Davies, B. (1990) 'The Social Production of Welfare and consumption of social services', *Journal of Public Policy*, Vol. 10, No. 3, pp. 331–47

Netten, A. and Smith, P. (1998) *Developing a Measure of Social Care Outcome for Older People. Interim Report.* PSSRU Discussion Paper No. 1487. Canterbury: Personal Social Services Research Unit, University of Kent at Canterbury

Netten, A., Dennett, J. and Knight, J. (1999) *Unit Costs of Health & Social Care 1999.* Canterbury: Personal Social Services Research Unit, University of Kent at Canterbury

O'Boyle, C.A., McGee, H.M., Hickey, A., Joyce, C.R.B., Browne, J., O'Malley, K. and Hiltbrunner, B. (1993) 'The Schedule for the Evaluation of Individual Quality of Life (SEIQoL), administration manual', Department of Psychology, Royal College of Surgeons in Ireland

Oliver, M. (1993) 'Disability and dependency: a creation of individual societies?', in J. Swain *et al.* (eds) *Disabling Barriers and Enabling Environments.* London: Sage Publications in Association with the Open University

Posnett, J. and Jan, S. (1996) 'Indirect costs in economic evaluation: the opportunity cost of unpaid inputs', *Health Economics,* Vol. 5, pp. 13–23

Qureshi, H., Patmore, C., Nicholas, E. and Bamford, C. (1998) *Outcomes in Community Care Practice. Overview: Outcomes of Social Care for Older People and Carers.* York: Social Policy Research Unit, University of York

Qureshi, H. (1998) *Overview: Outcomes of Social Care for Older People and Carers.* York: Social Policy Research Unit, University of York

Selai, C.E., Trimble, M.R., Rosser, M.N. and Harvey, R.J. (2000) 'The Quality of Life Assessment Schedule (QOLAS) – a new method for assessing Quality of Life (QOL) in dementia' in R. Logsdon and S. Albert (eds) *Assessing Quality of Life in Dementia.* New York: Springer

Discussion

The final part of the discussion was the most technical and it is difficult to avoid this (Sarah Byford's paper summarises the key definitions). Four main approaches were considered in the way that costs and effectiveness might be applied to implementing independent living in practice:

- cost-minimisation
- cost-utility
- cost-benefit
- cost-effectiveness.

Cost-minimisation was simply about achieving the lowest cost. *Cost-utility* was about a more holistic framework in terms of achieving a quality of life. *Cost-benefit* was about calculating all of the potential impacts of a given intervention. All of these were seen as problematic in some way. Cost-minimisation was, in many ways, the current mode of thinking that people found unsatisfactory. Cost-benefit was more 'whole system' in its consideration, but was more about decision making on individual projects (it was also rarely used in health economics, since it was difficult to put a monetary value on extra years of life or notions of 'independence'). *Cost-effectiveness*, on the other hand, looked at ways of achieving a single dominant outcome (or a variant of that, cost-consequence, looked at achievement of a few identified outcomes).

In the discussion, the groups agreed that, in the longer term, a focus on cost-utility (addressing a wide framework of quality of life) would be desirable, but the methodology here remained under-developed.

In the short term, it was more realistic to aim for cost-effectiveness, since it would be manageable to predefine one or two dominant outcomes to be achieved and then look at routes to achieving these.

It was agreed that it was important to start to develop frameworks that reflected the support that people received, the processes that informed the quality (or otherwise) of that support, and the outcomes from that support that people valued.

In the discussion, an exploratory framework was presented, within a flow diagram between boxes that covered costs, resource inputs, non-resource inputs, intermediate outputs and final outcomes (see Figure 6.2 in Chapter 6).

The model was a Social Production of Welfare (it was recognised in the discussion that, in the same way words within independent living had specific technical meanings, so did phrases like Social Production of Welfare within welfare economics).

It was important within this model to:

- measure social care outcomes which met user and carer needs

- recognise the basic inputs that go into producing support

- have clear rules of comprehensive measurement

- look at the variations between people and to compare like with like.

There were disagreements within the discussion about the specific elements within each box, but conceptually the approach was seen as possibly promising. Some of the disagreements on the elements within the boxes were less about economics and more about good process and outcomes within a value-base of independent living.

- For example, 'personal care' was presented as a basic commodity within the model. The group felt that this seemed actually to 'commodify' something. It was the complete antithesis of the Social Model of Disability and had a specific meaning within current practice about functional bathing, dressing, etc.

- More generally, many of the final outcomes were still seen as very functional. Independent living transcended these outcomes; user control of these (and other) 'commodities' could be seen as both a process and the primary outcome.

- There was some anxiety about the notion of someone being a productive unit. Some of the division here was that there were two approaches to 'equity'. The first was a welfare approach, where people's net contribution could be assessed in their contribution to society's well-being as a whole. The second was a rights-based approach, where people had rights which were not necessarily dependent upon their role in, or economic/materialist contribution to, society as a whole.

It was agreed that it is crucial both to identify the processes that are important within this model and to start to measure outcomes.

Conclusions

Going back to the three questions that the seminar was intended to address, the summary view of the group was as follows.

- In social care and disability issues, it is possible, indeed it is essential, to develop ideas of effectiveness that are centred on the lives and experiences of users of support/services. Philosophies such as independent living provide a strong basis for that, and one challenge is to include the diversity of experience of older people, disabled people, service users (including those from black and minority ethnic groups) in ideas of effectiveness.

- The ideas that underpin Best Value provide an opportunity for more robust formulations of cost-effectiveness to be taken forward. However, Best Value does not have all (or even many) of the answers as yet. The intellectual territory and implementation of cost-effectiveness that truly represents the views of users is still to play for.

- There are outline frameworks and modes of thinking within economics in general, and health and social care economics in particular, that have possibilities. It would be worth speculating on what a follow-up paper from an independent living economist might look like in three years' time.

These are the more general conclusions from the discussions. There were also some specific possible areas of work, which others (including the Foundation) might look to take forward.

Building blocks for cost-effectiveness and independent living

There was a need to develop ideas of the cost-effectiveness, consequences or utility of independent living. These might be given force by mapping out what one might expect independent living to achieve in practice. This could build on Ann Netten's framework to develop an understanding of independent living processes and outcomes. This might be taken further and then tested through an expert consultation. A later phase might be about research and development work to refine an approach in practice and develop its applicability and to carry out empirical work more robustly to test the usability of these ideas in practice.

Engaging with current policy issues

- Performance indicators need to be reviewed and refined. It would be good to derive more meaningful, practical short-term ideas which could indicate whether or not independent living was being achieved. Routine monitoring of the quality of service delivery should also be implemented in practice.

- Conversely, it would be important to identify performance indicators that were currently problematic and were actually indicators of irrelevant activity or had the potential to reward practice which limited independent living.

- It would be good to look at specific studies that could illuminate approaches and weaknesses. Three areas of investigation seemed ripe:
  1. Cost-effectiveness, independent living and charging policies
  2. Cost-effectiveness of support services and direct payments
  3. Cost-effectiveness and health gains of independent living (e.g. for people who use direct payments).

However, it was also important to recognise that robust measurement will in the longer term need substantial empirical evidence.